TAKE YOUR PET TOO!
Fun things to do!

by Heather MacLean Walters, PhD

M.C.E.
Chester, New Jersey

Cover illustration by Mari Graphics

Additional illustrations:
Bob Bates, Karen Bonner, William MacLean
Photography by Heather Walters
Cover Photo by Jeanne Conover

Printed in the United States of America

ISBN 0-9648913-1-X

DEDICATION

This book is dedicated to my grandfather, Paul West Maynard, who taught me to love and respect all living things, and to my grandmother, Alice Maynard, who gave me the courage to do very silly things and enjoy them.

ACKNOWLEDGMENTS

The author wishes to acknowledge the following people for their special contributions.

Karen Bonner
Bob Bates
Jeanne Conover
David MacLean (Sr.)
William MacLean

I'd also like to express my gratitude to all the people at pet-friendly establishments around the country who provided input, information, and encouragement for this effort. A special thanks to my hard-working husband, Rob, who provided inspiration at every turn. And finally, to Ted, whose wagging tail every time I pick up the car keys lets me know that all the work is worth it!

CONTENTS

Special Offers & Order Form

INTRODUCTION

"A violet by a mossy stone
Half hidden from the eye!-
Fair as a star,
When only one is shining in the sky."
-William Wordsworth
She Dwelt Among the Untrodden Ways (1799)

"Full many a gem of purest ray serene
The dark unfathom'd caves of ocean bear:
Full many a flower is born to blush unseen,
And waste its sweetness on the desert air."
-Thomas Gray
Elegy in a Country Churchyard (1750)

The world is full of a myriad of wonderful experiences! Feel the joy of just being alive and able to seek the 'violet by the mossy stone' or the 'gem of purest ray' hidden in a cavern or deep in virgin woodland. Take the time to look for the evening star. Take the time to love someone or some wonderful creature. And take your pet along! You'll both be better for it.

Welcome to a guide that's meant to give pet owners and their pets joy and satisfaction at vacation time. This guide was written so that we would be encouraged to take pets on vacation, to festivals, to concerts, and just about everywhere. The more we venture out with adorable, well-behaved pets, the more inroads we can make into exciting events and places. If we are responsible pet owners, we should be allowed to bring our pets anywhere without a fuss (look at Europe--they're way ahead of the U.S. in this respect!).

This is a guide to festivals, towns, beaches and anything else fun that is also pet-friendly. Included are adventures that are fun for humans (that also allow pets), adventures for pets (that also allow humans), and adventures for both.

There are literally thousands of hotels in the U.S. and Canada that accept pets, some of which are listed in this book. Should you need a more comprehensive list, please refer to the list of publications in the back of this guide.

Beware! This is a fun-loving, sometimes irreverent and serious guide to pet-friendly events in the U.S. I have endeavored to reach every type of interest (with a couple of exceptions-see below) from auto racing to tea-sipping. In the course of compilation, I found some events and places that I felt needed to be included for their humor or shock value. Only one of these events, in Minnesota, does not allow pets.

There are certain categories of events that are purposefully excluded because they do not foster the kind of humane treatment that we need to give to the other creatures that share this planet with us. Out of respect for the living beings of the earth, there is no specific listing of places to hunt, fish, or see circuses or rodeos. If that is what you like to do, you'll need to get that information elsewhere. Most dog shows are not included either because your pets are not always welcome; only pedigreed competitors are allowed. There are exceptions, however, like the friendly UKC in Michigan which welcomes any pet on leash. You may contact the AKC, UKC or local kennel club for more information. While this is not a vegetarian guide, most events are fairly animal neutral (except Montana) and fun is derived from activities other than inflicting pain.

Finally, keep in mind that the events in this book are but the tip of the iceberg for pet-compatible vacations. The resource guide in the back of this book provides other valuable sources of information for the pet lover. Ultimately, however, the list of possible trips is limitless - and growing larger all the time. I encourage you to explore other possibilities, using this book as a guide to what is available.

If your favorite pet-friendly travel destination isn't among those in this book, I'd encourage you to write to us at MCE and tell us about it A form for this purpose appears on the following page. Or if you prefer a more high-tech communication, drop us an e:mail at **Docmaclean@aol.com** or **Heather@world2u.com**. We'll send out a special gift for the best new vacation ideas!

Please copy this form, fill out, and mail to the address below.

MY FAVORITE PLACE TO TRAVEL WITH MY PET

Name: _____

Address: _____

City: _____

State, Zip: _____

Daytime Phone: (____) _____

Pet Name & Type: _____

Your Pet-Compatible
Vacation Spot: _____

What do you most like to do there?

_____

_____

What other pet-compatible activities are available in the area?

_____

_____

Are there nearby hotels that accept pets? Please provide names, addresses and phone numbers of contacts if they are available.

Please mail responses to: MCE, P.O. Box 84, Chester, NJ 07930.
Thanks for your participation, and happy travels!

FUN THINGS TO DO - A PREVIEW

In 1995, I completed Take Your Pet Along, a guide to hotels and motels that accept pets throughout the U.S. and Canada. I began that compilation for my own use, so I'd never have to worry about being stuck without a place to stay with my dog Ted. Friends and other pet lovers wanted copies, and before I knew it I was in the publication business. Thousands of people have used Take Your Pet Along for holiday travel, cross-country moves, or family vacations.

It seems, however, that in solving one problem, another appeared: now that you know where you can stay with your pet, what can you do with him or her once you're there? The thought of bringing your loved one on vacation, only to leave him or her in a hotel room, was at best a half-solution. That issue became the genesis for Take Your Pet Too.

Having conducted a fairly exhaustive campaign, and even so just scratching the surface of pet-compatible vacationing, a better question seems to be: is there anything you can't do? While you'll find some specific attractions off-limits to your pet, virtually any activity imaginable can be done somewhere with your furry pal in tow.

To illustrate this point, and get you started on your journey through this book, browse through the summaries of activities you can enjoy on the following pages. Additional information for these sites is provided in the body of the book, under the respective region and state.

Wouldn't you and your family really rather bring the pet with you? Well, now you can!

Selected Annual Festivals (Pets Welcome)

Bat Flight Breakfast...Carlsbad, NM
Food, Folks, and Spokes...Kenosha, WI
National Teapot Show...Creedmore, NC
Zuccini Festival..Eldorado, OH
Meteor Shower Camp...Waynesville, OH
Clown Town Colossal..Delevan, WI
French Festival of New England...............................Newport, RI
Mozart & Folk Art...Stowe, VT
Thunder In The Mountains....................................Wheeling, WV
Buzzard Day...Glendive, MT
Salute To Elvis Presley...Baltimore, MD
Share Cabarrus Fest...Concord, NC
Old Mill Days...Neligh, NE
Oil & Gas Festival.. Sistersville, WV
Pickle Fest...Atkins, AR
Peach Festival...Chester, NJ
Pumpkin Show...Circleville, OH
Potato Festival..Henager, AL
Pecan Festival..Okmulgee, OK
Huntsman World Senior Games............................St. George, UT
Howl-O-Ween..North Branch, NJ
ESPN Extreme Games..Newport, RI
Art On The Green..New Castle, DE
American Folk Life...Washington, DC
Jackson Boat Show..North East, MD
Bayou Razz-Jazz Fest...Mt. Airy, MD
Table Settings and Garden Boutique.........................Hohokus, NJ
Movies Under The Stars...Hoboken, NJ
Isle of Wight County Fair......................................Smithfield, VA
Sweet-Tea Sip Off...Mobile, AL
The Rose Festival...Thomasville, GA
The Blues Fest...Helena, AR
Branson Music Fest...Branson, MO
Church Point Buggy Festival...........................Church Point, LA
Covered Bridge Festival.......................................Madison Cty, IA

Great Movies/TV You Can Relive

Mystic Pizza...CT
The Witches of Eastwick..MA
Ghost Busters...NY
Annie Hall...NY
Manhattan..NY
On The Town...NY
Seinfeld...NY
Mad About You...NY
The Odd Couple..NY
King Kong...NY
Ground Hog Day...PA
Reversal Of Fortune..RI
The Great Gatsby...RI
Forest Gump..DC
1776..VA
Breaking Away..IN
Lonesome Dove...TX
Gunsmoke..TX
Bad Girls...TX
Texas...TX
Streets of Laredo...TX
The Alamo...TX
Interview With The Vampire..LA
The Bridges of Madison County...IA
Field Of Dreams..IA
Dances With Wolves...SD
North By Northwest...SD
Return Of The Jedi..CA
Lethal Weapon..CA
Mash...CA
Star Trek IV..CA
Close Encounters Of The Third Kind.....................................WY
Beethoven...MT

Dog Camps (people allowed too!)

Camp Gone To The Dogs..Putney, VT
Dog Scout Camp...Swans Creek, MI
Dog Days of Wisconsin...Dousman, WI
Canine Camp of the Redwoods.......................Boulder Creek, CA
Legacy Training Camp...Moscow, ID
Wiz Kid Dog Camp..Morgantown, PA
Camp Winnaribbun...Reno, NV

Selected Dog-Friendly Beaches

Acadia National Park..Bar Harbor, ME
Wolf's Neck..Freeport, ME
Winslow Memorial Park...Freeport, ME
Sea Point Beach..Kittery, ME
Commercial Street Beach................................Provincetown, MA
National Seashore...Truro, MA
Mirror Lake..Lake Placid, NY
Lake Placid (Boat Launch)...................................Lake Placid, NY
Cape Henlopen State Park...Southern DE
North Fenwick Island State Park................................Eastern DE
Higbee Beach..Cape May, NJ
Cape May Point...Cape May, NJ
North Wildwood..North Wildwood, NJ
South Lake Drive...Lakewood, NJ
Ocean County Park...Lakewood, NJ
Cape Hatteras National Seashore....................................All of NC
Atlantic Beach..Atlantic Beach, NC
Isle of Palms..Charleston, SC
Hilton Head...Hilton Head, SC
Lake Athens...La Rue, TX
Port Aransas...Port Aransas, TX
Delmar Beach..Carmel, CA
Pismo Dunes..Southern CA
Astoria Beach...Astoria, OR
Seaside Beach...Seaside, OR
Cannon Beach...Cannon, OR
Tilamook Beach..Tilamook, OR
Lincoln City...Lincoln, OR

Pet Fairs & Festivals

Connecticut Pet & TICA Cat Show............................Hartford, CT
American Spaniel Club.....................................Marlborough, MA
Dogs Walk Against Cancer....................................New York, NY
Long Island Pet Expo..Uniondale, NY
Pet Fair..Long Island, NY
New York Pet & AACE Cat Show..............................Suffern, NY
Rhode Island Pet & CFF Cat Show........................Providence, RI
March For The Animals.......................................Washington, DC
Annual Bark Ball..Washington, DC
St. Hubert's Giralda Dog Walk...................................Madison, NJ
Pet Fair..Mountainside, NJ
Polo & Pooches Dog Show...Revere, PA
Memorial Weekend Classic Dog Show................New Castle, PA
Christmas In July/Portraits....................................Smithfield, VA
Dog Days Contest...Smithfield, VA
Blessing of the Animals..Smithfield, VA
Annual Dog Mart...Fredricksburg, VA
Dog Festival...Fredricksburg, VA
Annual Reindog Parade...Charleston, WV
Ft. Lauderdale Pet Show..................................Ft. Lauderdale, FL
Cat Fanciers Association..Naples, FL
Pet Industry Christmas Show...................................Rosemont, IL
Cat Fanciers Association..Chicago, IL
Chicagoland Family Pet Show......................Arlington Heights, IL
Cluster in the Hills..St. Clairsville, OH
Dayton KC Show...Dayton, OH
Memorial Day Cluster..Hamilton, OH
Art Show at the Dog Show...Wichita, KS
Krewe of Barkus..New Orleans, LA
Tri-City Dog Show...Davenport, IA
Basset Hound Picnic..Arcadia, CA
American Family Pet Expo...Pomona, CA
Feast Of Lanterns..Pacific Grove, CA
International Pet Expo...Las Vegas, NV

Superlative Pet-Friendly Events

Largest Cast Metal Sculpture..............................Birmingham, AL
Oldest Law School in the U.S.................................Litchfield, CT
Most Recognizeable Driveway.................................Vacherie, LA
Largest Storytelling Fest...Murray, KY
Largest Peanut Boil..Luverne, AL
World's Largest Pecan Baked Item........................Okmulgee, OK
World's Longest Breakfast Table........................Battle Creek, MI
World's Largest Wizard of Oz Fest........................Chesterton, IN
World's Largest Buffalo.......................................Jamestown, ND
World's Largest Corn Maze...Fargo, ND
Most Witchy Place..Salem, MA
Largest Dinosaur..Cabazon, CA
Oldest Dog Festival..Fredricksburg, VA
Only U.S. Tea Plantation.....................................Wadmalaw, SC
Longest Frame House.................................Sherwood Forest, VA
Oldest Cave...Childersburg, AL

Seconds
Second Best Spa in U.S...Telluride, CO
Second Largest St. Patrick's Parade.......................Savannah, GA

<u>Create Your Own: In Pet Friendly Towns</u>

Pretzels..Lancaster, PA
Animated Film..Kissimmee, FL
Dolls..Litchfield, CT
Pottery..Creedmore, NC
Starring Role...Pidgeon Forge, TN
Jewelry..North Creek, NY
Elvis..Baltimore, MD
Crazy Boat...Asheville, NC
Gift Baskets..Freeport, ME
Earrings...Provincetown, MA
Clown..Delevan, WI
Dog Costume..New Orleans, LA
Yell..Dardanelle, AR

TRAVEL TIPS FOR PETS

Traveling with pets really is less difficult than traveling with children. A little advance planning will go a long way toward making your trip more enjoyable for both you and your furry pal. The following are some common-sense "do's and don'ts" for ensuring a trouble-free vacation you'll all enjoy.

First, a warning: many of the establishments we've visited lately have instituted stricter pet policies or are considering not allowing pets. This has come about because of one or more bad experiences with pets barking, scratching, biting, or going where they're not permitted. Needless to say, the fault here lies with the owners, not the animals. We owe it to our fellow pet owners to abide by the rules so that more and more hotels and attractions will welcome rather than shun pets. Please do your part to make animals (yours and everyone else's) welcome!

Getting Ready

Here are a few ideas we've found to make our Ted's trip (and hopefully your pet's) less stressful.

First, ask yourself if your pet is really ready for a trip. If you've never taken your pet on a trip before, you may want to start with overnight or weekend excursions rather than throwing Fido headlong into a three-week cross-country marathon. Overall health and temperament are also issues to be addressed. Pets prone to car sickness, pets with current illnesses, or pets that misbehave and are destructive may be best left at home.

Once you're convinced that your pet can handle the trip, start packing! Bring the pet's normal food; changing diet while on a trip can cause distress or illness. Bring plenty of treats to reinforce good behavior. We use larger numbers of smaller treats while on travel, so Ted can be rewarded frequently. And pack some of your pet's favorite toys (let him help with this task if he's so inclined).

Other important items to bring: ID tags; medications; medical records (in case of emergency); collar & leash; bed or cage (if applicable); food and water dishes; pooper-scooper; and a supply of water (we usually keep a gallon jug in the trunk in case we're far from a water supply).

On the Road

When traveling by car, plan on stopping every few hours to walk your pet. Breaking up the trip is a good idea even without a pet, but with a pet in tow it is a necessity. We look for rest areas at approximately two hour intervals, though your pet may require more or less frequent stops. A dog will begin to get restless when he needs to relieve himself, but it's best to start looking for a place to stop well before this happens.

Allow enough time for the pet to relieve itself and get some exercise. Pets also get dehydrated during travel, so bring water and allow your pet to drink before moving on.

When at a rest stop or other unfamiliar area, make certain your pet is leashed at all times. The potential for accidents is simply too great to leave your pet off leash even for a moment at a rest area.

Finally, if you're pet is not a seasoned car traveler, don't try to cover huge distances in a day. You'll only end up at your destination tired and frustrated. If your destination is much more than four to six hours away, consider stopping at an intermediate point. If you pick your stopover points carefully, you'll find that getting there really is half the fun!

In the Air

Great news! If you have a dog or cat that is 25 lbs. or less and can fit under your seat, you may take him/her in the cabin with you on most major carriers (call first)!! *Someday, the airlines will let us all take our well-behaved pets in the cabin.* This is an important consideration because of the vagaries of the hold where they are kept during the flight.

It can get hot (or cold) enough to kill or give brain damage to any animal on very extreme days. Pilots monitor the temperature, but there's not a lot they can do about it. I have to give credit, though, to all the pilots (like that British Air pilot recently) who are willing to temporarily abort a flight to save an animal life. In this British Air case, I understand the hold temperature was approaching a murderous 120 degrees Fahrenheit. On his way overseas, the pilot noticed and stopped the flight in Boston to get the animal help. God bless him.

Air travel can be particularly stressful for animals and owners alike. There are a few things you can do. First, give your pet plenty of water about four hours before departure time (depending on the length of the flight). Walk the pet 30 to 60 minutes prior to takeoff (always). This way the pet will be hydrated enough, but will not have to relieve itself during the flight. You may want to line the pet's cage with some soft material in case he gets jostled about.

In the heat of summer it is best to take an evening flight or a short early morning one, to prevent the pet from getting overheated. In the winter, the opposite applies; take day flights or short afternoon flights to alleviate the cold. Remember your baby might get left on the tarmac for a while the other luggage is being loaded. Be mindful of the temperature. Always try to get a non-stop flight to prevent other mishaps too.

Opinions are mixed on whether to give animals a mild sedative prior to traveling. My personal opinion is that it's a bad idea, because such drugs may impair reaction time and make an animal more prone to injury in the event of turbulence. If your animal is very high-strung though, he may need something to relax. You should discuss this matter with your veterinarian before embarking.

Certain airlines have special arrangements for passengers traveling with pets. They will take special care of your pet, making sure all is well with Fido or Fifi. Each airline calls it something different, but you need to make arrangements well before you leave.

At the Hotel

Within this guide you will find hundreds of hotels, motels, B&Bs and resorts that (as of press time) will welcome you and your pet. There are other guidebooks (such as Take Your Pet Along) with more exhaustive listings. No matter which source you use, <u>always call ahead</u> to confirm that the place still accepts pets, as ownership changes hands frequently and policies may change on short notice. Don't try to sneak a pet into a hotel or motel - it only lowers the odds that the establishment will ever accept them.

When you make your reservations, let the representative know that you're bringing a pet, and provide details when requested. Some hotels have limits on the number and/or size of the pet allowed. Because an alternate pet-compatible establishment can be hard to come by on short notice, seriously consider guaranteeing your reservation for late arrival. (We learned this lesson the hard way, and suggest that you not repeat our mistake.)

Once at the hotel, set up a special place that your pet can identify as his/hers; crates, beds, toys and what-have-you should go in this spot. Give your pet some time to explore the room and get comfortable with the new surroundings. Set food and water bowls on easy-to-clean floors (preferably not on a carpeted surface).

Hotels that accept pets can be valuable pet travel information sources. Not surprisingly, proprietors that allow pets are often current or former pet owners themselves, and they often have a wealth of information on local parks, beaches, and other attractions where you'll be able to take the pet along. They may also have information on veterinarians and animal hospitals in the event of an emergency.

If you have to leave the pet in the room unattended, hang the "Do Not Disturb" sign on the front door. You don't want the housekeepers walking in on an animal without advance warning. Some hotels require you to notify the front desk if a pet is left unattended; observe this rule if it applies.

Try not to leave the pet alone in a hotel room for very long. This can be stressful for an animal - after all, the pet has no way of knowing that you'll ever return. Leave the pet with a treat, maybe the television on low, and a sincere promise to return soon. If pets learn to associate your leaving with a treat, it becomes more pleasant for them. When you do return, praise your pet and spend some time with him/her to provide reassurance that your excursions will be temporary ones. Remember, the whole point of the book is to bring the pet whenever possible, so hopefully you won't need to leave him/her very often.

Out and About

Once you're at your destination, you'll want to get out and explore the territory. So will your pet. Once again, the common sense/common courtesy rules apply. Keep your pet leashed at all times. Clean up after your pet, whether or not it appears to be required. Carry water with you, and let your pet drink frequently.

Although you've heard it a million times, let me offer reminder one million and one: **do not leave your pet unattended in a hot car.** Every summer, dogs and cats die needlessly because people didn't think it was that hot or that they'd be gone that long. When the outside temperature reaches 75 degrees, the temperature inside a car can exceed 100 degrees only minutes after you park. If you must leave an animal in the car alone, park in a shady spot, leave the windows open, and return within 10 minutes.

A similar rule applies in winter. Though most dogs are fairly tolerant of the cold, prolonged exposure (especially if your dog is unaccustomed to severe weather) could be dangerous. Less protected areas such as the feet and face are especially prone to the cold. For winter outings, consider outfitting your pet with appropriate protective gear, sold in most pet shops.

Well-behaved pets are welcome in many shops, particularly in towns which cater to tourists. Always ask first. By shopping in pairs, one person can always wait outside with the pet while the other shops.

Eating with a pet in tow can be a little tougher, but in the summer, many restaurants with outdoor seating will let your pet sit with you. Keep your pet on a short lead under these conditions, to avoid unfortunate incidents involving food at adjacent tables! Another pleasant alternative is to pick up sandwiches or other picnic-style food and eat at a nearby park or town green.

Many dogs love to swim and will take to the water at a moment's notice if you let them. We always carry a spare towel in case Ted locates a choice spot for an impromptu swim. Use judgment in selecting swimming venues: especially avoid stagnant water (may harbor organisms which carry disease) and rivers with strong currents. Observe posted rules when they exist. Bodies of water which feed public drinking supplies are generally off limits to all swimmers, both human and canine, so abide by the rules. Monitor your dog closely at the beach and make sure his enthusiasm doesn't get him in "over his head", so to speak. And don't let him drink salt water - bring a fresh water supply with you.

The Scoop

Remember to pick-up after your pet, especially if he/she does his/her business in a public place. You want to be able to take your pet *more* places, don't you?! We must be mindful of the *Homo sapiens*' fear of dog poop! We mustn't frighten them. Squirrels, rabbits, birds and other critters doing their thing and grown men tinkling on highway signs and relieving themselves in bushes on camping trips all are acceptable, but dog doody is not. We must conform in order to help the cause, so please scoop! Remember for me, it's "Doody-Free"!

HEALTH TIPS FOR HOME & TRAVEL

Pets provide us with much entertainment and affection. We care very much about their welfare. This section strives to give suggestions so that your pet will have a healthy, happy life. First let's look at food issues, and then chemical, cleanliness and social issues.

Dog Food

At the present time, the most efficient way to make sure your dog has most of the proper nutrients is to feed him any of the good standard dog foods. Make no mistake, the dog needs *dog* food! Much of the discussion that follows is about carefully choosing the right dog food and making other wise choices about feeding and caring for your dog.

Reading Labels
The food we feed our pets differs from owner to owner, and with all the choices out there now, it's no wonder it's hard to know what's good or bad for our pets. We read the ingredients on our own food labels, but do we read pet food labels regularly? No, probably few of us think we have the extra time. Isn't it worth the time, though, to insure that your pet does not get cancer, diabetes, or even worms? Expenses aside (and disease is expensive!), the agony of watching a pet suffer through a traumatic illness is more than some people can bear. We can prevent a lot of this unnecessary distress if we have a little bit of knowledge.

Colors and Flavors
Pet food is often a lower quality *of people food* that is highly processed and, as such, needs extra enhancement to make it appear and taste palatable. Among the chemicals used to achieve this palatability are artificial colors and flavor. It is wise to look at each package of treats or food and determine just *how much* coloring or artificial flavoring is present before you buy it for your dog. Less is better. This is not difficult, just look at the food and you'll be able to tell if it's extra red, yellow or blueish. This is not to say that all colors or flavors are bad, just that consuming *excessive* amounts of any colors or artificial flavors is not a good idea.

In order to tell approximately how much of a given substance is found in any food (people or pet food) you must look at the list of ingredients. The first ingredient listed is the most abundant ingredient in the food. The rest of the list is in order of actual amount found in the food. So, for example, if the last ingredient listed is a food additive, you know that of all the ingredients that are in this formula, the food additive is found in the smallest amount. This general formula applies to all foods.

Preservatives
While absolutely necessary to keep certain foods from spoiling, it is also certain that some ingredients have been found to precipitate cancer. **BHA** and **BHT** have long been controversial. They are effective as antioxidants in food with fat content (they prevent the food from spoiling), but they have been implicated in cancerous events in animals. Look for them in you own diet as well as your dog's. And don't be fooled about the phrase, "BHA added to packaging". There is a migration of this chemical into your food. It was moved to packaging to quell the fears about it being in food, but it is still there.

People Food
What about "people food"? **What is "people food"?** "People food" is just a better grade of the very same ingredients and substances which are over-processed in dog food. Read the dog food ingredient labels. Is any ingredient in dog food something you wouldn't find somewhere in people food? No. It's all food that could be eaten by people who consume over-processed food. Animal fat preserved with BHA or beef tallow for example (that we see in several dog foods) can be found in baked goods! Table food, known for years as "people food" is not inherently bad for dogs and it gives them a much needed change from the same boring dog food every day. The major caveat about people food is to **beware of over-feeding your dog.** Feed them only proper people food such as examples from the list below.

The place you run into trouble is when your diet is not a good one and you feed the dog what you eat. Contrary to conventional wisdom, dogs do not need high fat, extra beefy diets. "But they're carnivores" is the typical response. They might be carnivores, but they benefit from vegetable and carbohydrate matter as well. Carnivores in the wild often eat the intestines of their (herbivore) prey as a means of obtaining pre-digested vegetable matter. Dogs no longer live as carnivorous hunters; they eat dry grain substances as a staple of their diet. Just read the label on your dry dog food. Isn't corn or rice listed among the first three ingredients in the label?

Begging Dogs
Before dogs were domesticated, they used to run free and forage all day for food. Now they are kept in a box, a house, or a confined outdoor space and can no longer hunt for their food. Primal panic set in, and they quickly developed a method to obtain food when they could not go look for it; begging. A begging dog is not a bad dog, anymore than a crying baby is bad. Both have desperate needs to fill and you are the only source of fulfillment. You do need to remember, however, that the dog should not be given food *ad libitem* all day long. Sometimes dogs do not know when they have had enough to sustain them. Beware of overfeeding them.

The dog may also beg just to acquire some of the better quality food that you're eating. Can you blame him? You might now say, "I feed him all the time...why is he begging?" He is begging because **he does not know**, due to the very unpredictable nature of the human, **whether you will ever feed him again.** "Oh, that's silly..." I hear you saying. No, actually it isn't. Think about it. He can't talk, open the fridge, go in the cupboard, or call for take-out. Sometimes you disappear without warning for hours at a time (to work, shop, etc.). There is a very uncomfortable feeling that sets in when you don't know when or if your **only** source of food, water, bathroom relief, companionship, personal care (for fire, accidents,etc.), will come back. Have you ever forgotten to feed him? There's a panic situation for a dog. Dogs only understand so much; they might wonder if they did something wrong so you've decided to starve them, or they might think you need a reminder. We expect a lot from dogs behavior-wise, but we need to understand them or we'll never get what we want out of them.

If you want to prevent your dog from using his natural instincts at the dinner table, I have a couple of suggestions. First, **feed him before you eat dinner.** This allows him to relax a bit about foraging, and it makes you feel less guilty when you don't give him food directly from the table. Secondly, **do not give him any**

food while you're sitting at the table. It won't take long before he gets the hint. Lastly, the suggestion that has worked well with my dog, is that I **always share everything else with him**. If it is a food that he shouldn't have a lot of, he only gets a sniff and a lick (or a very small portion). But he feels so confident that I will give him some of whatever I have that he has stopped begging for it. He always gets that last little piece of bagel or last lick of my ice cream. He trusts me. And that is more important than anything else.

Scraps

Sometimes we like to give the dog leftovers. This can be a good thing if the leftovers are foods that we ourselves would eat and if they are not excessively fatty, sugary, or salty. After all, the dog laps them up with relish. It is not, however, a good idea to give the dog something that you would not consume. Food that is not fit for consumption can contain or create **nitrosamines**, **epoxides**, and many other toxic or carcinogenic substances; these potentially pre-cancerous compounds should be avoided by both human and animal. Nitrosating substances (such as compounds which are precursors to **nitrosamines**) are known to create precancerous conditions in the stomach when ingested regularly. **Epoxides** are oxides of the fat in old food and are formed especially in dry food like crackers and biscuits (both for humans and dogs). Bacteria, fungi and viruses can also be found in leftovers. Old dog food (both dry and moist) should be discarded and never fed to your dog. If you feed old food to your dog, you are asking for trouble in the form of chronic disease. When in doubt, throw it out.

Cleanliness

It is important to keep your dog clean and dry. This may sound like common sense, but sometimes it is not. Dogs do not need to be bathed excessively, occasionally will do (see your veterinarian for specific amount). Make sure you use shampoo made for dogs, or one that has a lot of conditioner in it, because you can dry out the dog's coat with human products. But it needs to be stressed here that exposure to different and large numbers of microbes due to a dirty living situation can precipitate long-term disease and disability. Certain viral diseases can predispose human individuals to cancer. It does not take a great leap to suppose that this might occur in dogs as well.

Flea/Tick Chemicals

Flea and tick dips, sprays, and collars can be both toxic and carcinogenic to pets and people. The precautionary statements on the packaging should be enough to distress the average owner, but the fear of fleas often outweighs any worry we might have about the contents. This needs to be addressed. Finding a viable alternative (like Pennyroyal oil,etc.) should be a goal of each pet owner.

Fleas can also be stopped with cleanliness. Vacuum bags can be sprayed with anti-flea chemicals and then all flea eggs and larvae swept up from rugs and floors. Bedding should be changed frequently and laundered well.

Ticks are another story. No matter what collar or preparation you use, your dog can come back to you with a tick or two. All the lawn chemicals and the other chemicals serve to do is kill off the beneficial insects; you'll still see some ticks unless your yard is very enclosed. There is no easy answer.

Eating Grass

Dogs eat grass for different reasons. Prior to domestication, dogs used herbs and grasses for fiber, nourishment and for medicinal purposes. Grass often serves as a emetic, making them regurgitate, a defense against toxic substances or bad food. Grass may also serve as a source of chlorophyll, fiber, or any of a number of things yet unknown to us. If your dog is eating grass, there's probably a good reason for it. Before stopping him, ask yourself why he's doing it - and then consider asking the vet.

Barking Dogs

Barking dogs are insistent. Some consider them annoying. But do you know what a barking dog is doing? **He's talking!!!** He may be saying, "For God's sake bring me in out of this rain or cold!" OR "There's someone trying to take our territory!" OR "I'm hungry, thirsty, in need of exercise, dying in this heat, etc.... have some pity!"

Remember, most dogs do not speak just to listen to themselves. They have an important message. Listen to your dog (and others). You could learn a lot!

Violent Dogs

Dogs are not naturally violent. Violent dogs should not be blamed for the criminal actions of their human owners. They should not be "put down" after an incident. We should rehabilitate them after removal from the owner. It is the owner who needs to be punished, not the dog.

Caging

Caging is necessary when traveling with major airlines, possibly for early training, taking cats to the vet, or as a temporary solution when an animal might be hurt or hurt others. It is not meant as a permanent home for an animal. All the major zoos in the world know this; they've developed aviaries instead of caging birds in cramped quarters, and all animals previously confined to small spaces are now given habitats. It is only the dog population that still suffers from a lack of humane living quarters.

Dogs are very social animals. Unfortunately, they are often left in cages to sit, alone all day long, for the rest of their lives, because the owner is unable to get proper training. **Think what we are doing to them!** I know those of you who purchased this guide understand what I am about to say, so share it with your pet-owning friends and neighbors. This book is designed to give alternatives to leaving and caging a pet.

Contrary to popular thought, **Dogs don't like cages. People do**. A cage is open on all sides and not a "safe" environment to live in. Any great general will tell you that he'd never be willing to put his troops into such a completely vulnerable situation (open for attack on all sides). It's indefensible.

An animal will, however, go into a cage if it knows the owner wants it to; what choice does it have? An animal will also come rushing out of a cage like a crazy person if it's been in there all day long. It is much easier on owner and pet if the pet has a little freedom all the time. A pet is less prone to misbehavior if left out of the cage and trained properly with love. Dogs fare much better with a little daily socialization and play. So let those caged animals out!

Stress

We all experience stress at one time or another, and we know that stress can precipitate major illness and even some cancers, but do we think about the stress our pet might be under? "Not very often", would be the typical answer. Well, consider the following, and then think of some simple steps that you can take to save yourself several hundred dollars in vet bills and make your own and your pet's life better.

We tear them from their real families forever, giving puppies a metal noise-making device (alarm clock) that they must pretend is their mother's beating heart so we don't have to listen to them crying in the night. We tell them not to talk to any members of their own species, and scream at them when they do. We drag them around in choke chains, short leashes, pinch collars, use elaborate electrical shock devices, force them to drink only water, and eat the same tasteless, boring food for the rest of their lives. How would you feel if that were you? Would you still be man's best friend? Think long and hard and try and empathize. It is a very important exercise. We need to do better.

We can do better. If dogs were more accepted in public, maybe their sorry lot would change a little. In its own way, this guide is trying to create opportunities for freedom and enjoyment for both owner and dog.

There is no question that pet ownership is a responsibility to give affection to, play with, and care for another creature. It has been shown that pets that are given such affection and adequate play time are much less prone to the ravages of serious disease. Following the advice of a good veterinarian and these few simple suggestions can make your life (and your pet's life) much easier and happier.

1. **Read labels on dog food.**

2. **Supply your dog with alternatives** such as carrots, broccoli, fruit, or whole grain breads. (Note: not all dogs will like all vegetables/fruit; they each have their own preferences. Don't force your dog to eat anything it doesn't want.)

3. **Look for dog food that is not over colored.**

4. **Look for dog food that has few artificial preservatives or additives.**

5. **Look for a dog food that is lower in fat**; this will lower the amount of preservatives needed to keep this fat from spoiling.

6. **Eat better yourself.** If you eat better foods, like whole grains and fresh fruits and vegetables, your dog will benefit from your fresh leftovers.

7. **Throw out old food, both the dog's and your own.**

8. **Purchase from a busy or reputable grocer.** A busy grocery store is a sign that the food turns over fast and is probably fresh. It is also a sign that people are pleased with the food quality.

9. **Train your dog with operant conditioning.** Train your dog with reward for good behavior and not too much punishment for bad. He will learn more quickly and you will both have less stress.

10. **Get help.** Find a puppy play class if you're not home during the day. Send him/her to puppy school for training so that he/she can stay outside the cage when you are not home. Ask a neighbor (perhaps a retiree or a mother home with kids) to stop and visit your "friend" once a week. People who are without adult company often relish any change in their regular routine. You will be helping your lonely neighbors as well as your pet.

CHANGING THE WORLD FOR THE BETTER

It's easy to have a good influence on the earth. *You alone* can make this a better place than it was before you arrived. We should all strive to do that; it's one of the standard practices of responsible earth-stewardship. Not only can you control any land you have or what you do when you visit land that's not your own, you can help any living creature with which you come in contact.

Here are a few suggestions:

Save the Butterflies and Eliminate Ticks

No one wants his or her dog to have ticks. A few options are available. The standard pesticides sold in the hardware store offer only temporary solutions because they work only for a few days, killing the beneficial insects, and then the ticks are back. And, in spite of what is on the packaging, we cannot now be sure that the Lyme Disease organism (*Borrelia burgdorferi*) is found only in the deer and the white footed mouse population and is eliminated with these applications. It is now assumed to be in any warm blooded woodland creature, so the ticks have even bigger sources of disease to choose from.

Pesticide use around the home and outdoors is dangerous to you, your children, the pets, and the butterflies! What is the answer? There are several:

- Do not use yard or bug killing chemicals.
- Remove ticks with tape after you walk your dog.
- Keep the lawn mowed low; ticks love tall grass.
- Give your dog an herbal or low-toxic tick collar.
- Plant a beneficial insect garden away from the house.
- Vacuum (in the house)all the time; and thoroughly.
- Weed your garden by hand.
- Guinea hens--the Billy Joel solution (they love ticks).

Save the Endangered Bird Species

To help the warblers and other imperiled species, be a good land steward. Get involved with your town planning board; go to meetings, become a member, write letters to them and local editors about local land development and habitat preservation. And look to your own backyard. Once again, don't use insect killing chemicals--the birds eat insects! Leave that ugly old bush in the backyard if you ever notice birds in it. Don't chop down that tree; it could be good habitat for several species. Preserve sources of clean water. **AND KEEP THE CAT BELLED!!!** Thrushes and other ground dwelling birds and mammals are decimated by loose unbelled cats. That little noise might alert one of these increasingly rare birds to fly up just before it becomes a victim.

Save a Dog or a Cat Life

There are several humane organizations that sponsor dog walks for the benefit of unlucky or abused animals in shelters. Several are listed in this guide. If you do not see one in an area in which you live or visit, you have two options; call all the local humane societies and ask if they sponsor such a walk or start one yourself!

One of the nicest things you can do is to help out at your local humane organization. If there is nothing they need you to do on site, you could buy them dog or cat food, blankets, toys, or treats. Drop by for a Christmas or Hanukah visit and bring some cheer (or some treats) to the poor, impounded creatures. Donate funds and receive a tax deduction. Combine saving the earth from excess waste with helping the animals and convince a local restaurant to donate all of their leftover food (still fresh but unsaleable) to the local shelter as a treat for the furry residents.

Adopt a friend. Or convince someone else to adopt. A good family is made better by a loving relationship with a pet. Be good to your two and four-footed friends; they try so hard to please you.

Save a Human Life

Fido and Fifi can save a human life along with you. Not by an unusually heroic effort, but by walking in an American Cancer Society "Dogs Walk For Cancer" event. (See New York City). There are walks like this all over the country; AIDS walks, MS walks, etc. If you don't see it in this guide, call your local societies or start one yourself.

USING THIS BOOK

The body of this guide, listing pet-compatible activities across the U.S., is divided into eight geographic regions: Northeast; Mid-Atlantic; Southeast; Midwest; South-Central; North-Central; Southwest; and Northwest. Within each region, states are arranged alphabetically.

Addresses, phone numbers, and basic directions are provided for places and events to help you plan your vacation. You should contact local event organizers for the most up-to-the-minute details. Note that the dates of specific events vary from year to year, so you will want to call ahead to make certain your trip coincides with the event.

For each state, we have included a representative sample of lodgings which will accept pets. This book is not designed to be an exhaustive listing of available accommodations, nor does inclusion in this book constitute an endorsement of any particular location. An order form for Take Your Pet Along, a more comprehensive hotel/motel guide for travelers with pets, can be found in the back of the book.

Codes for amenities and costs of the hotels in this book are as follows.

Hotel Cost Codes (for average one-night stay)

*	$30-60/night
**	$61-100/night
***	$101-150/night
****	$151 and up/night
W	Hotel has weekly rates only

Note: costs may vary by season.

Hotel Amenity Codes

A   Airport nearby
H   Handicapped access
HS   Hair salon on premises
G   Golf within 10 miles
NS   Non-smoking rooms available
OB   Facility is on the beach
P   Playground on premises
R   Restaurant on premises
S   Swimming on premises
SA   Sauna on premises
SK   Skiing within 25 miles
T   Tennis within 10 miles

As a final reminder, pet policies are often subject to change with little or no advance notice. When planning your trip, please make sure to confirm pet policies in advance, particularly for lodging.

NORTHEAST

NORTHEAST

NORTHEAST

Connecticut
Maine
Massachusetts
New Hampshire
New York
Rhode Island
Vermont

Hotel Cost Codes (for average one-night stay)

*	$30-60/night
**	$61-100/night
***	$101-150/night
****	$151 and up/night
W	Hotel has weekly rates only

Note: costs may vary by season.

Hotel Amenity Codes

A	Airport nearby
H	Handicapped access
HS	Hair salon on premises
G	Golf within 10 miles
NS	Non-smoking rooms available
OB	Facility is on the beach
P	Playground on premises
R	Restaurant on premises
S	Swimming on premises
SA	Sauna on premises
SK	Skiing within 25 miles
T	Tennis within 10 miles

NORTHEAST

NORTHEAST
Connecticut

Sights/Towns To See
Mystic Seaport
Mystic is an historic representation of daily life in a New England fishing village in the 1800's. There is a large maritime museum on the site as well. Dogs on leash are welcome on the grounds and even in some of the exhibits (including the museum), but not in the restaurants. Don't panic if you see the "NO DOGS" sign right on the harbor--it's for the restaurant! People need to be reminded that the restaurant is off limits. Several large colonial ships are docked in this village and available for boarding. There is currently a steamboat ride up the Mystic river that dogs are allowed on as well.

Relive the movie "Mystic Pizza" by dining at the real restaurant (sans chien) where Julia Roberts met her friends, or visit Ford's Lobsters a few towns over in Noank. You'll recognize nearby Stonington as the site of the filming of "Mystic Pizza". Check out the Groton/New London submarine base; tour the inside of an actual submarine! (Sorry, no dogs inside this one) Groton, London and Mystic are easily accessible off I-95.
Mystic Pizza (860) 535-3700
Mystic Seaport (203) 572-0711
Mystic Chamber of Commerce (860) 572-9578

Hotels/Motels

Howard Johnson Lodge	Amenities: R	Cost: **
Exit 90 off I-95		
Mystic, CT		
(203) 536-2654		
Oakdell Motel	Amenities: R	Cost: **
983 Hartford Rd.		
New London, CT		
(203) 442-9446		

Red Roof Inn   Amenities: R   Cost: **
707 Coleman St.
New London, CT
(203) 444-0001

Litchfield/Farmington
One of the oldest towns in Connecticut, Litchfield boasts lovely walks, restaurants and private gardens. Home of America's first law school, still standing on South Street in town, Litchfield retains its 18th century charm. Take a stroll on Main Street along the village green and explore the charming cafes like the West Street Grill, the gardens and 18th century houses. Aspen Garden Restaurant has an amazing take-out menu with well over a hundred items to choose from for romantic evenings or picnics. Browse in the cute shops for curios and antiques. Visit nearby White Conservation Center with its 4,000 acres of wildlife sanctuary and activities. There are endless lovely trails and the pooch can swim in several places. Canoeing, hiking, biking, fishing, and strolling humans with dogs are found everywhere. Eat a wonderful light dinner at Grappa just outside of the Litchfield Common; they accomodate your pet as best they can while they serve you great fresh fish and Italian dishes.

One of the more interesting places in the Litchfield area is the Susan Wakeen Doll Company. Here you can make your own doll! And Fido can watch, if he's well behaved and you'll pick up after him! There are several different models to choose from, dozens of dresses, shoes and hairstyles. You pick the head, arms, and legs and they'll help you put the doll together. Then it's on to the hair and outfits. Lots of fun, especially for that little girl who gets to design her own special friend.

Farmington is also a lovely 18th century town. Complete with exquisite straight front colonial homes which are traditional white with black shutters, Farmington has lots of beautiful things to see. Antique shops abound in this and adjacent communities, and there are lots of good restaurants. While the Toll Gate Hill has lovely, well appointed rooms with a Williamsburgish colonial decorative flair; the Centennial has much more in the way of amenities (fireplace, kitchen, microwave, unbelievable room service, exercise room, pool, etc.). Peaceful and relaxing, both towns make great getaways.

Hotels/Motels
Toll Gate Hill Inn   Amenities: R, SK   Cost:***
Route 202 (P.O. Box 1339)
Litchfield, CT 06759
(203) 567-4545

Red Bull Inn   Amenities: H,R,S,T,NS   Cost: *
300 Schraffts Drive
Waterbury, CT 06705
(203) 597-8000

The Centennial   Amenities: R,S,G   Cost: **
5 Spring Lane
Farmington, CT 06032
(203) 678-1000

Festivals/Happenings
Antique Carriage Rally (October)
Litchfield
A must-see event with costume and riding competitions and an antique horse and carriage exhibition. The second Sunday of October each year at White Memorial on Route 202 (See above).

Antique Carriage Rally
(203) 775-3223

Apple Harvest Festival (October)
Southington
Baked goods, arts and crafts, and a parade and carnival accompany the festivities. Outside on the town green, people and pets stroll and take in all the entertainment.

Apple Harvest Festival
(860) 225-3901

NORTHEAST

Cheshire Historical Society Antique/Craft Show (September)
Cheshire
Arts and crafts are the focus of this festival which combines a museum exhibit with heritage and historical items of interest. Use the phone number below to inquire about the **New Britain Dozynki Festival** (Local cuisine, dancing, ethnic exhibits, etc.) the **Cheshire Fall Festival** (Horse show,horticultural exhibits, fair, stage shows, etc.), and the **Berlin Fair** (carnival, horse competition, food and drink, and live entertainment)

Central Connecticut Tourism
(860) 225-3901

Haddam Neck Fair (August)
Haddam Neck
Lots of art, including modern, folk and contemporary crafts can be found at this fair. Livestock competitions (I want to go just for the "talent" part--will the pianist or the baton twirler win this year?) and related farm events accompany the artwork at this full event.

Haddam Neck Fair
(860) 267-4671

Chester Fair (August)
Chester
Every August on the Chester Fairgrounds, this large combination fair, horticultural, horse, livestock, folk art and educational event takes place. The Fairgrounds are located on Middlesex Turnpike. I was told that pets have been allowed there in the past.

Chester Fair
(203) 526-2315

Walking Weekend (October)
Mansfield Hollow Dam Park hosts this walk for canines on Sunday after all the human weekend walking activities are finished. Another way to meet friendly dogs and their owners!

NORTHEAST

Walking Weekend
Northeast Visitor's Center
(203) 928-1228

Connecticut Dressage Association-Horse Show (June)
Simsbury
Contact:
Ms. Sharon Knies
42 Whalers Point
East Haven, CT 06512
(203) 777-3637

Hotels/Motels
The Simsbury 1820 House   Amenities: R   Cost: **
731 Hopmeadow Street
Simsbury, CT 06070
(203) 658-7658

Farmington Horse Show
Farmington, CT
Contact:
Mrs. Jan Smith
92 Stagecoach Rd.
Holliston, MA 01746
(508) 429-5410

Hotels/Motels
The Centennial   Amenities: R   Cost: **
5 Spring Lane
Farmington, CT 06032
(203) 677-4647

Connecticut Pet Show and TICA Cat Show (November)
Hartford Civic Center
Hartford, CT 06103
(203) 563-2111

NORTHEAST

Hotels/Motels

Ramada Inn Cap. Hill 1   Amenities: H,R,NS   Cost: *
440 Asylum St.
Hartford, CT 06103
(203) 246-6591

Econo Lodge   Amenities: R   Cost: *
927 Main St.
E. Hartford, CT 06108
(203) 289-7781

Camping Information
Bureau of Parks and Forests
165 Capitol Avenue
Hartford, CT 06106
(203) 566-2304

Maine

Sights/Towns To See
Bar Harbor
Beautiful coastal scenery is the hallmark of any visit here. The name, "Bar" Harbor, comes from a unique geographical occurrence at low tide in the harbor. There is a lovely unspoiled island that can be seen from the pier where the sunset cruises and whale watching boats are docked near the edge of town. This island is inaccessible until low tide, when a sandbar, wide enough to walk across, forms long enough to allow access on foot. Take your furry friend, but be careful: the tide comes back in a lot faster than you expect and you could be stuck there for several hours.

Stroll along the main streets and back roads; everything in town is within walking distance. Dozens of little antique, clothing, sports, and new age knick-knack shops and restaurants (The Italian Fisherman, The Dog House, The Jordan Pond House, and Beal's Lobster Pier were happy to accomodate our friend for lunch or dinner) delight even the most jaded of shoppers. Fido may even be allowed in many of them, but please ask first. We found that Domus Isle, The Blueberry Patch, Acadia Shops (there are 5 of them) and others were glad to have leashed pets visit while we shopped. Several galleries including the Birdsnest Gallery on 12 Mt. Desert Street were pet friendly. The Birdsnest is a first-rate collection of stunning paintings at reasonable prices.

Take your pet for one of the most lovely drives in the U.S., through Acadia National Park. See northern pine forest that wends itself to the edge of rocky cliffs covered in morning mist. See vistas that stretch for miles and lovely mirror lakes. Both of you can walk up Cadillac Mountain, a challenging but not incredibly difficult walk to a peak with a great view. Rent a canoe on Long Pond and see the sights from the water (with your pet, but be careful).

Pets are welcome on leash in most areas of the park. In the very heart of the park are many activities-horseback riding, dining (you can get great takeout and sit on the lawn overlooking the lake in one of those famous Maine/Adirondack chairs with your pet by your side), spelunking (there are some neat caves-you have to look for them), and climbing (a peak called Precipice has always been my favorite, but there are health warnings at the bottom that you should heed). You can climb Precipice only if the peregrine falcons aren't nesting at the time. They have priority, as they should.

There is an unusual cameraderie between visitors to this coastal town that has to be experienced. Everyone is friendly and there's lots to see and do. You can even bank (!) with your pet at pet-friendly First National on Main Street or at Bar Harbor Banking and Trust. We met lots of people on a sunset cruise with wine, dinner, and my Ted on a lovely three-masted, red-sailed schooner called The Natalie Todd. It was the perfect cap to a wonderful vacation in lovely Bar Harbor.

Acadia National Park Tours (207) 288-3327

Hotels/Motels
Days Inn   Amenities: G,H,T   Cost: **
SR 3
Bar Harbor, ME 04609
(207) 288-3321
(800) 325-2525

Balance Rock Inn   Amenities: R, S   Cost:***
21 Albert Meadow
Bar Harbor, ME 04609
(207) 288-9900

Bar Harbor Inn   Amenities: R, S   Cost:***
Newport Drive
P.O. Box 7
Bar Harbor, ME 04609
(207) 288-3351

Wonderview Inn   Amenities: R, S   Cost:***
SR 3
Bar Harbor, ME 04609
(207) 288-3358

Additional Motels
Kelley's Cottages   (207) 288-3129
Rose Eden Cottages   (207) 288-3038
Hanscom's Motel   (207) 288-3744
Ocean Drive Motor Ct.   (207) 288-3361
The Ryan Estate   (207) 288-5154

Bar Harbor Campgrounds
Hadley's Point Campground   (207) 288-4808
Mt. Desert Narrows   (207) 288-4782
Spruce Valley Campground   (207) 288-5139

Sights/Towns To See

Kittery

Home of dog-friendly beaches, ocean views, and lots of outlets. There are so many major brand outlet or discount stores in Kittery that, along with the scenery, you may never get to visit them all. The discounts on items that you'd normally buy are so great, that most people leave with a moundful of treasures. **Please do not leave the dog in the car!** You'll forget, in those heated or air-conditioned stores, that a poor creature is suffering outside. Instead, take turns shopping (note: there isn't much shade either) or leave him at your dog-friendly hotel with a family member. If you're careful, Kittery can be fun for everyone. You can always come home at the end of the day with a big treat for your special friend!

The Big Dog sports shop welcomes dogs (especially BIG ones!) and you can eat at the wonderful Chauncey Creek Lobster Pier with your friend. A full lobster dinner with Fido! We enjoyed the view, the food and the service. Walk your dog on Seapoint Beach after 5 P.M.--- everydog who's anydog is there and running FREE! Fort Foster at

Kittery Point and York Cliff also allow your dog on the beach. Explore lovely historic downtown Portsmouth, New Hampshire which is a stone's throw away from Enchanted Nights. Walk around with your pooch and then dine on great cuisine at Cafe Brioche in the heart of New Market Square.

Hotels/Motels
Kittery Motor Inn   Amenities: R,S   Cost: **
Rt. 1 Bypass
Kittery, ME 03904
(207) 439-2000

Enchanted Nights   Amenities: R   Cost:***
29 Wentworth Street
Kittery, ME 03904
(207) 439-1489

Freeport
Patronize familiar friends in outlet form like LLBean, Dexter Shoes, Ralph Lauren, Patagonia, Calvin Klein, etc. Pets are not allowed in all the stores, though. I guess they're not as open-minded as NewYork City (later in guide--check it out!)... LLBean has a shady place for you to tie them up and a water dish for them, though. One of the fun places we also found in Kittery was the Big Dog Sporting Goods outlet. They love to have dogs visit, and have lots of dog paraphernalia (tee shirts, etc.) Clothing stores abound in this shopping mecca, but other types of items can be purchased in the Crabtree & Evelyn and Wilbur Chocolate outlets. In all there are about 110 shops. Stop at The Lobster Cooker restaurant for lunch and dine under the umbrellas with your friend or get take out for you and the pooch at Crickets or any of dozens of take-out places in town.

If you're staying at the Isaac Randall House--you can walk to town and avoid the parking nightmares. It also might be best to leave him in the hotel for a short while if you're traveling solo and planning to shop for several hours. Otherwise you can switch off shopping and dog-entertaining with your traveling partner. Wolf's Neck is the local park where you can walk your friend and he can swim!

Freeport Inn   Amenities: R   Cost:***
335 US 1 South
Freeport, ME 04032
(207) 865-3106

Isaac Randall B&B   Amenities: R   Cost:***
5 Independence Dr.
Freeport, ME 04032
(207) 865-9295

Festivals/Happenings

Fall Foliage Festival (October)
Boothbay Harbor
Look for the full-size, narrow-gauge railroad engine out front to let you know you've reached the Fall Foliage Festival and Railroad Village Museum. Arts and crafts, an antique auto museum, music, food and drink accompany this homage to the reds and yellows of fall.

Fall Foliage Festival
Boothbay Civic Association
P.O. Box 81
Boothbay, ME 04537
(207) 633-4924

Bowdoin Summer Music Festival (June)
Brunswick
Pets are allowed on the Bowdoin College Quad at the Family outdoor concerts. They are also allowed at the concerts on the Green. This festival lasts throughout the months of summer and many concerts are given by top name performers, though not all are pet-friendly.

Bowdoin Summer Music Festival
36 Greenridge Ave.
White Plains, NY 10605
(914) 664-5957

NORTHEAST

Dog Friendly Beaches
SeaPoint/ Kittery
Ogunquit Cliff Walk/Ogunquit (after Oct 30)
York Cliff Walk/York
Fort Foster/Kittery
Fort Gerrish/Kittery
Prescott Park/Newcastle
Odiorn State Park/Kittery
Wolf's Neck/Freeport

NORTHEAST

Massachusetts

Sights/Towns To See

Boston
From the Freedom Trail Walk through the heart of Boston to the Boston Common, there are lots of fun things to do with your pet. Newbury Street boasts very trendy and posh shops as well as cute cafes and eateries and makes a very pleasant walk. Some of the outdoor restaurants do not mind you sitting and eating with your dog. Boston Common is a continual streetfest of artists, musicians, actors, and regular folks (with their dogs!). Bring a blanket and a lunch from one of the many eateries adjacent to the Commons and watch the action.

Of all the hotels listed, The Four Seasons and The Ritz Carlton will treat your dog as someone special. The Four Seasons has a pet menu with "Barnyard Chase" (a chicken dish with corn) and "Rin Tin Tartare" (steak & potatoes) for dogs. For cats there is The Cat's Meow (poached salmon), Cat Nap Sack (scrambled eggs with ham & cheese), and Kitty Seafood Buffet (salmon, tuna, and whitefish); all are served with steamed white rice.

Hotels/Motels
The Four Seasons   Amenities: R   Cost:****
200 Boylston St.
Boston, MA 02116
(617) 338-4400

Ritz Carlton   Amenities: R   Cost:****
15 Arlington St.
Boston, MA 02117
(617) 536-5700

Howard Johnson Hotel   Amenities: A,R,S,NS Cost: **
200 Stuart St.
Boston, MA 02117
(617) 482-1800

Boston Harbor Hotel   Amenities: R   Cost:****
70 Rowes Wharf
Boston, MA 02110
(800) 752-7077

The Charles Hotel   Amenities: R,S   Cost:***
One Bennett at Eliot St.
Cambridge, MA 02138
(800) 882-1818

Lexington/Concord
The birth of our independent colonies, these United States, took place
in this historical crucible. Stroll downtown Lexington's cobblestoned
main street, visit the wonderful chocolate shop as you head toward the
Minute-Man statue. Explore the small craft and gift shops before you
head to Concord. In Concord you'll find similar shops and many more
large, historical homes. Look for the bridge where it all began: "By the
rude bridge that arched the flood, their flag to April's breeze unfurled.
Here once the embattled farmers stood and fired the shot heard 'round
the world".

In this same dog friendly area you'll find homes of some of our
greatest thinkers and writers. Emily Dickinson's home, Walden Pond
(the home of Henry David Thoreau), Harriet Beecher Stowe, Ralph
Waldo Emerson and Henry Wadsworth Longfellows' homes, etc. Visit
the Colonial Inn downtown and lunch, pet and all, on the veranda.
Further west in Sudbury you find the historical Wayside Inn which
featured prominently during the early days of our country.

Hotels/Motels
Howard Johnson Lodge   Amenities: H,R,S,NS   Cost: **
Route 2 & Elm St.
Concord, MA 01742
(508) 369-6100

Battle Green Inn   Amenities: N/A   Cost: **
1720 Massachusetts Ave.
Lexington, MA 02173
(617) 862-6100

The Colonial Inn   Amenities: R   Cost: ***
48 Monument Square
Concord, MA 01742
(508) 369-2170
(800) 370-9200

Salem/Gloucester
Witches, warlocks, and widows walks adorn this wonderful historical
area filled with beautiful ocean views, lovely victorian homes, cute
shops and Nathaniel Hawthorne's gabled abode. The Salem Witch
House and Witch Museum tours have tales of accusation, hysteria and
betrayal to share, and Laurie Cabot who was head of NOW (National
Organization of Witches) has run an interesting little shop in the
downtown district for a while. If you're at all interested in the
atmosphere that witchcraft has brought to the area, the best time to go
is during Halloween. All the shops stay open almost all night,
everyone is costumed in wild and brilliant creations, there is a haunted
house set up in town and a costume ball given at the Salem Inn. To get
into the mood, watch "The Witches of Eastwick" with Bette Midler,
Cher, and Jack Nicholson; it was filmed in Salem. **Do not take your
pet into the haunted house or anywhere there are loud noises that
would frighten him/her.**   Dogs don't seem to like Halloween or
costumed people, but a walk in the sea mist by the Hawthorne house
before the festivities begin might be nice for your pet.

Hotels/Motels
The Salem Inn   Amenities: R   Cost:***
7 Summer Street
Salem, MA 01970
(508) 741-0680

The Stephen Daniels House   Amenities: R   Cost: **
1 Daniels St.
Salem, MA 01970
(508) 744-5709

NORTHEAST

Sturbridge

Old Sturbridge Village was 50 years old in 1996! It has always been a wonderful recreation of life in the early 1800's. Period costumes adorn every staff member and they run this village just as it would have been run long ago. You'll find the village smithy, "his large and sinewy hands" running the forge, fresh loaves of bread baking in stone dutch ovens, and a civilized version of "the tragedy of the commons" as the pigs, goats and chickens share the village green for grazing. It's all here and so much more! Among the 20-30 festivals each year in the town (where the antiquing is great), the village itself, and the Public House less than a mile away, are **Mystery weekends**, **Magic shows** (1820's style), **New England Wedding Day**, etc. The fun never ends. (I spent part of my honeymoon here so I'm partial to the whole area.) Don't forget the incredible **Brimfield Antiques Show** in May, July and September. All the above welcome your dog on leash.

Old Sturbridge Village
1 Old Sturbridge Village Road
Sturbridge, MA 01566
(508) 347-3362

The Publick House Motor Lodge   Amenities:R,G   Cost:**
Route 131
Sturbridge, MA 01566-0187
(800) PUBLICK

Cape Cod
<u>Sights/Towns To See</u>
Provincetown

Wild and wonderful Provincetown is a shopping and activities mecca. Seashells, crafts and clothing, ice cream and home-made taffy, great jewelry and earrings, charcoal portraits by local artists and lots to do like the maritime museum, visiting the dunes, nature walks at the National seashore fill the days with fun. The beach on Commercial Street allows dogs, but it isn't a big beach for sunning, just enough for allowing Fido to taste the salt air and frolic. Visit the fragile dunes in North Truro and look for signs of life in the sand, like camouflaged speckled birds eggs or small invertebrate skeletons. Nearby Wellfleet

(15 minutes away) has a big flea market at the drive-in on Route 6 that is worth checking out (every Wed.).

Hotels/Motels

The White Wind Inn   Amenities: N/A   Cost: **
174 Commercial St.
Provincetown, MA 02657
(508) 487-1526

Hargood House   Amenities: OB   Cost: W
493-A Commercial St.
Provincetown, MA 02657
(508) 487-9133

Chatham/Orleans

Chatham is a quiet town with nice clothing shops, craft shops, and ample opportunities to stroll along peaceful streets or dine at pleasant cafes and restaurants. Go to the pier and watch the fishing boats come in with their catch of the day; it should supply you with food for thought.   In Orleans you can find little shops, sailboats to rent, rowboats to fish from, a minor league baseball team you can watch at night, and several good fish restaurants. Drive along main roads and look at the lovely Cape architecture. There are hidden activities in every corner of these two little towns.   Friendly Morgan Cottages allows your dog on the beach and has wonderful private homes for you to choose from. Every summer Saturday in the park on Main Street there is a live jazz, rock or big band for listening or dancing.

Hotels/Motels

Morgan Cottages   Amenities: S,T,OB   Cost: W
444 Old Harbor Rd.
Chatham, MA 02633
(508) 945-1870

Skaket Beach Motel   Amenities: S,T   Cost: ***
Route 6A
Orleans, MA 02653
(508) 255-1020

Nantucket

Quiet private place that caters to clientele who like it that way.
Clothier Tommy Hilfiger is currently building a house out here. Hop
the ferry with your pooch and have a nice rest. Beautiful beaches, fine
dining, 2 public golf courses on an island only 4 miles wide and 10
miles long. Bicycle paths go everywhere and there is no crime. Ah...

Hotels/Motels
10 Hussey Street   Amenities: N/A   Cost:***
Nantucket, MA 02554
(508) 228-9552

The Grey Lady   Amenitiers: N/A   Cost:***
34 Center Street
Nantucket, MA 02554
(508) 228-9552

The Boat House   Amenities: N/A   Cost:***
15 Old North Wharf
Nantucket, MA 02554
(508) 228-9552

Festivals/Happenings

Cape Cod Dressage-Horse Show(June)
Buzzard's Bay
Contact:
Ms. Wendy Le Shan
21 Beechwood Rd.
Centerville, MA 02632
(508) 771-1681

Hotels/Motels
Bay Motor Inn   Amenities: R,T,OB,G,P   Cost: **
Route 6
223 Main St.
Buzzards Bay, MA 02532
(508) 759-3989

NORTHEAST

Dillingham House   Amenities: R,OB   Cost: **
71 Main St.
Sandwich, MA 02563
(508) 833-0065

American Spaniel Club (July)
Best Western Royal Plaza
Marlborough, MA
(706) 860-0881

Hotels/Motels
Best Western Royal Plaza   Amenities: R   Cost: ***
181 Boston Post Rd.
Marlborough, MA 01752
(508) 460-0700

Super 8   Amenities: R   Cost: **
880 Donald J. Lynch Blvd.
Marlborough, MA 01752
(508) 460-1000

Dog Friendly Beaches
North Truro/North Truro
Marconi Station/Welfleet (Fire roads)
Commercial St./Provincetown

New Hampshire

Sights/Towns To See

The White Mountains
750,000 acres of New Hampshire beauty await the avid hiker, biker or fisherman. Beautiful trails, vintage mansions, and covered bridges can be found in this region. Drive up the east coast's tallest peak and you can adorn your car with the popular bumper sticker, "This car climbed Mount Washington". It is a tough climb for any vehicle, and a breathtaking view at the top. If you are a birder you'll want to catch migration. Both raptors and warblers can be seen in abundance, though sometimes there are a lot of people at the summit and it is adviseable to go a bit lower for optimum viewing.

Hotels/Motels
Maple Leaf Motel   Amenities: SK   Cost: **
Box 917
Route 16
North Conway, NH 03860
(603) 356-5388

Eastgate Motor Inn   Amenities: SK   Cost: **
RFD 1
Littleton, NH 03561
(603) 444-3971

Castle in the Clouds
Moultonboro
Home of Castle Springs bottled water and brewery, this castle was built by wealthy financier Thomas Plant. The Ossippee Mountain Range serves as "the Clouds" for this wonderful home. The dog can tour the grounds and picnic with you, but he can't tour the castle, brewery or water bottling facility.

Castle in the Clouds
(603) 476-2352

Friendly Farm
Dublin
Even if you don't go, you have to make the phone call to hear the recording. It's a farm right in the center of town, complete with pigs and chickens, etc. Pack a picnic lunch to eat there, but, as the pig says about your sandwich, "Please don't make it ham!"

Friendly Farm
(603) 563-8444

Franconia
"Two roads diverged in a yellow wood..." "Whose woods these are I think I know..." Understand the motivation and see the "yellow wood" in fall or the woods that "fill up with snow" near the home of Robert Frost.. Visit The Robert Frost House on Ridge Road and stroll the nature trail he frequented while creating his many wonderful works. A tour of the house and small museum includes a slide show about his life. See Franconia Notch, take the tram up Cannon Mt. Great hiking can be found in Franconia which is about 1 hr. from Mt. Washington.

The Robert Frost House
Franconia, NH 03585
(603) 823-5510

Hotels/Motels
The Hilltop Inn   Amenities: R,SK   Cost: **
Main St.
Franconia, NH 03585
(603) 823-5695

The Horse and Hound Inn   Amenities: R,SK   Cost: **
205 Wells Rd.
Franconia, NH 03580
(603) 823-5501

Festivals/Happenings

Granite State Morgan Horse Show
Deerfield Fair Grounds

Deerfield, NH
Contact:
137 Main St.
Hampstead, NH 03841-2038
(603) 329-5741

Hotels/Motels
Econo Lodge   Amenities: G,R,T,SK   Cost:**
Gulf St.
Concord, NH 03301
(603) 224-4011

Howard Johnson   Amenities: A,R,S,NS   Cost:**
298 Queen City Ave.
Manchester, NH 03102
(603) 668-2600

Dog-Friendly StateParks/Camping
Dept. of Resources
(603) 271-3254

Androscoggin Park
Annett Wayside Park
Bear Brook (Camping)
Chestefield Gorge
Coleman State Park
Crawford Notch (Camping)
Dixville Notch
Franconia Notch (Camping)
Greenfield State Park (Camping)
Mollidgewock State Park (Camping)
Mt. Sunapee

New York

Sights/Towns To See

New York City

Relive the scene from "Ghost Busters" in Lincoln Center, an "Annie Hall" or "Manhattan" scene near the Brooklyn Bridge, Cary Grant's frustrated meeting with Deborah Kerr atop the Empire State Building , or the fun of "On The Town" with Gene Kelly and Frank Sinatra. Watch your favorite old movie to get you in the mood for your trip to New York City.

Perhaps you have a favorite episode of "Mad About You" or "Seinfeld" that you'd like to relive. Figure out where "Murray" takes his walk.

Walk your dog in Central Park, attend an auction at Christie's at Park Avenue, hike down wonderful 5th Avenue and... **Surprise!** You can shop **IN** Bloomingdales, Tiffany's, Eddie Bauer, Lord & Taylor, Bergdorf Goodman, Saks and many more!!! As one who loves to shop, but hates to leave my best friend, this was great news! Check out The Banana Republic and Paul Stuart Clothiers as well.   Need to placate a child? No place is more fun than F.A.O. Schwartz, one of the largest toystores in the world. They always have interactive displays and exciting gifts. But wait. It gets better.

So you don't like to shop...perhaps you prefer a quiet afternoon of reading a favorite book but forgot to bring one with you on this trip. Never fear, Barnes & Noble, B. Dalton, Madison Avenue Bookshop, and The Dog Lover's Bookshop **all** allow your pet!!

Feeling hungry?   Visit the several pet-friendly restaurants...Chez Jacqueline, Tutta Pasta, Barking Dog Luncheonette, Sign of the Dove, Mr. Chips ice cream stores and many others!

Kenneled pets can ride city buses and subways. Yellow cabs are required to pick up people with pets. But just try and flag down one of these guys and you'll be glad there are limos and cabs specifically for pets that will whisk you off to your chosen destination. To entertain your pet with pet things, head for the Pet Department Store (West 54th St.), the largest pet store in NY. They will massage and entertain your dog. Hotel Pierre greets Fido with a personalized biscuit, room service and toys.

Hotels/Motels
The Carlyle   Amenities:R   Cost: ***
35 E. 76th St. & Madison Ave.
NY, NY 10021
(212) 744-1600

The Waldorf Astoria   Amenities:R   Cost: ****
301 Park Ave.
NY, NY 10022
(212) 355-3000

The Pierre   Amenities:R   Cost: ****
2 East 61st St.
New York, NY 10021
(212) 838-8000

Class Act Limousine   (212) 491-5300
Pet Cab   (212) 491-5313

Lake Placid
Nestled in the heart of the Adirondacks you can find the home of the 1980 Winter Olympics. See the Olympic Arena, the Olympic village, and all the marvelous facilities for athletes. Watch world class athletes prepare for competition. Three ice rinks and a ski jump are among the facilities left over from the Olympics a few years ago. Gift shops and restaurants abound in this quaint village.

Hotels/Motels
The Stagecoach Inn   Amenities: R,G,SK   Cost: **
370 Old Military Rd.
Lake Placid, NY 12946
(518) 523-9474

NORTHEAST

Ramada Inn   Amenities: R,G,NS,S,SK   Cost: **
8-12 Saranac Lake
Lake Placid, NY 12946
(518) 523-2587

Fleischmanns
Delaware & Ulster Vintage Train Ride (All Year)
Take a lovely one hour train ride in a restored vintage train (with your
dog) through bucolic Ulster county, after which you can hike in the
Catskill Mountains on any of the trails. Visit local flea and farmers
markets, and then eat out (in summer) at any of the many restaurants in
the town of Fleishmanns. River Run proprietor Larry Miller and his
pal Ruffian welcome all well-behaved owners and pets. Take-out is
also available at most restaurants, so you can bring your dinner home
to River Run and dine on the veranda with your pet. In the winter there
is cross-country skiing, downhill and a variety of winter sports. A
happening place!

Hotels/Motels
River Run   Amenities: R,G,NS,SK   Cost: **
"The Inn for Pet Lovers"
Main Street
Fleischmanns, NY 12430
(914) 254-4884

North River/Adirondack Mountains

You can ski in the winter at Gore Mountain, but did you know that on the back face of this mountain awaits a treat for you and your pet in the warmer months?! So he's been annoying you by digging up your best flowers and always trying to make himself a cool spot in the newly seeded grass? Put those talents to use in New York's only garnet mine. This event is for "finger-digging"patrons only, the female proprietor told me. No tools; but she didn't say anything about my extra helper...Hmmmm...He's welcome on this tour and boy can he dig...Hmmmmm...

Barton's Garnet Mine
P.O. Box 400
North Creek, NY 12853

Route 28
North River, NY 12856
(518) 251-2706
(518) 251-2296

Hotels/Motels
Garnet Hill Lodge   Amenities:N/A   Cost:**
13th Lake Rd.
North River, NY 12856
(518) 251-2821

Ithaca/The Finger Lakes

Ever since I was an undergrad "far above Cayuga's waters", there has been a rumor that some wealthy alumnus left funding for Cornell with the stipulation that no dog on campus be leashed. Rarely having seen any dog on campus with a leash (only running loose) I assumed that everyone had taken this to heart. Although I can't confirm the rumor, it's a nice thought and a stunning campus.

There's more to see and do at Cornell, the loveliest of all Ivy league campuses, than just about anywhere else I can think of. (No, I wasn't an English major). The variety in architectural styles alone will keep you entertained, but there is serious artwork at the Johnson Art Museum and in the older buildings like Goldwyn Smith Hall. Great lawns on each of the quads allow peaceful picnicking with Fido. There are many musical, theatrical, sporting, campus, and goofy fraternity events every month of the year. One of my favorite goofy events is the **Phi Psi 500** where participants dress up as M & Ms, knights, tablesettings, and fruit (and in other bizarre costumes) and run from business to business in college town.

Dogs are allowed or insinuated into just about every event. Only Willard Straight keeps them out of the dining area. In the summer there is **The Ithaca Festival**, a wild, dog-friendly melange of arts, theatre, and odd happenings that will delight (confuse) the festivalgoer. Don't miss the **Madison-Bouckville Antique Show** on Route 20 outside of Syracuse in August every year (pets are occasionally allowed). Visit the twin towers on the other side of the lake at Ithaca College. Great food, film and musical events come from this, Rod Serling's favorite school, Ithaca College.

I musn't forget what most people find exciting about this Finger Lakes town itself. The gorges! They are incredible! Everywhere you venture in Ithaca you can find some link to the gorges. Peaceful and relatively unsullied, you can tour them all with your dog. Large, lovely Cayuga Lake offers canoeing, sculling, water-skiing and other water delights. Bird on the water at downtown Stewart Park as you walk your pooch. Visit the Lab of Ornithology, famous to birders and twitchers around the world. [Note: Collegetown Motor Lodge is one of the many lodgings that you can go with a pet and **PAY HALF PRICE!!!** See the Pet Care Savings Club in the Pet Related Services Section in the back.]

Hotels/Motels

Collegetown Motor Lodge   Amenities: G,T Cost:***
312 College Ave.
Ithaca, NY 14830
(607) 273-3542
(800) 745-3542

Howard Johnson Lodge   Amenities: G,T,NS Cost:***
2300 N. Triphammer
Ithaca, NY 14850
(607) 257-1212

Ramada Inn Airport   Amenities: G,T,R Cost:***
2310 North Triphammer
Ithaca, NY 14850
(607) 257-3100

Festivals/Happenings

Long Island Pet Expo (November)
Nassau Coliseum
Uniondale, NY
(516) 889-6000

ASPCA Dog Walk (October)
Rumsey Playfield
Central Park, NY
(212) 876-7708

Pet Fair (October)
Franklin Square
Long Island, NY
(516) 785-1880

New York Pet Show and AACE Cat Show (April)
Rockland Community College
Suffern, NY
(203) 563-2111

Hotels/Motels
Econo Lodge   Amenities: G,R,T,SK   Cost:**
E. SR 59
Spring Valley, NY 10977
(914) 623-3838

Dogs Walk Against Cancer (May)
American Cancer Society
New York, NY
(212) 586-8700

K-9 Day
Yorkville Station
P.O. Box 6480
New York, NY 10128

Dog Lover's Bookshop
9 West 31st St.
Greeley Square Station
NY, NY 10001-0006
(212) 576-4333

Hotels/Motels
The Carlyle   Amenities:R   Cost: ***
35 E. 76th St. & Madison Ave.
NY, NY 10021
(212) 744-1600

The Waldorf Astoria   Amenities:R   Cost: ****
301 Park Ave.
NY, NY 10022
(212) 355-3000

The Pierre   Amenities:R   Cost: ****
2 East 61st St.
New York, NY 10021
(212) 838-8000

NORTHEAST

Rhode Island

Sights/Towns To See

Newport
The Newport Mansions

Let's face it, you can't leave Newport without at least a glimpse of the mansions. Pets are allowed on the cliff walk between the ocean and the homes, but not allowed in the homes. The walk alone is magnificent; three miles of beach and posh homes to dream about owning. In the fall, just before Halloween, a series of mystery dinner theatres are held in several of the mansions to get you in a festive, if ghoulish, mood. Pets are welcome on the beaches around the mansions before or after sunbathers have arrived or given up (respectively).
Newport Visitor's Bureau
23 America's Cup Ave.
Newport, RI 02840
(401) 849-8048
(800) 326-6030

Hotels/Motels

Comfort Inn	Amenities: G,H,R,S	Cost:**
936 W. Main Rd.		
Newport, RI 02840		
(401) 846-7600		

John Banister House	Amenities: G	Cost:**
56 Pelham St.		
Newport, RI 02840		
(401) 846-0050		

Festivals/Happenings
French Festival of New England (June)

Genuine festival similar to those given in the French countryside. French country fair, culinary workshops, cultural and sporting events. The woman who organizes this, when asked about the presence of pets said, "Absolutely!". I was also told that in a traditional French fair there are always vendors of pets/pet products and that they are welcome.

French Festival
Newport, RI
(401) 683-1479

ESPN Extreme Games (June)
Seven days of unusual and challenging sporting events, such as barefoot skiing, wakeboarding, sky surfing, bicycle stunts, etc. A must see for those who love sports, and your pet is welcome at almost every event. This year it is in Rhode Island, but it may move around the country.

ESPN Extreme Games
Newport/Providence, RI
(401) 274-7230
(860) 585-2000

Newport Jazz Festival (Summer)
The best jazz festival on the East coast, it is truly a shame that pets are not allowed on the grounds, but fear not, there are a number of places outside the actual grounds that you might be able to enjoy the music with your pooch for free. The atmosphere in and around the city is really exciting as well.

JVC Jazz
P.O. Box 605
Newport, RI 02840
(401) 847-3700

Rhode Island Pet Show and CFF Cat Show (March)
RI Convention Center
Providence, RI
(203) 563-2111

Hotels/Motels
Providence Marriott   Amenities: R,T,S   Cost:***
Charles & Orms St.
Providence, RI 02903
(401) 272-2400

Summer Concert Series By The Water (July)
A mixed blend of different styles every Tuesday in the summer. Jazz at the Beach, Fiddlers Two, the US Air Orchestra, Narragansett Bay chorus, a Country western band, and the Navy band all share their talents with locals and tourists alike.

Summer Concerts
55 Brown Street
North Kingston, RI
(401) 294-3331 ext.241

Annual Blessing of the Fleet (June)
Narragansett Bay blessing of the privately owned boats docked in the harbor. A dock party celebration held by three local restaurants follows the blessing. Your pet may partake of all of the festivities with you and I hear that the clam chowder is out of this world.

Annual Blessing of the Fleet
East Greenwich Cove
Water Street
East Greenwich, RI
(401) 884-6363

Hotels/Motels
Holiday Inn   Amenities: R,T,S   Cost:**
801 Greenwich Ave.
Warwick, RI 02886
(401) 732-6000
(800)-HOLIDAY

Vermont

Sights/Towns To See

Woodstock
Ski Okemo or Killington in the winter, hike Mt. Tom or canoe nearby, or just explore this lovely New England town that has so much to offer. There is a town green to stroll, and a covered bridge to admire (a must in quaint old New England towns!). Take your walks in Faulkner Park. For the Vermont dairy fanatic, Ben & Jerry's factory is only an hour away in Waterbury! The Inn of choice is The Kedron Valley Inn. Filled with charm and period pieces, it also boasts a great restaurant.

Hotels/Motels
Kedron Valley Inn   Amenities:R   Cost:***
Route 106
South Woodstock, VT 05071
(802) 457-1473

Topnoch at Stowe
Resort and Spa
Stowe, Vermont

Stowe
Ski one of the best resorts in the U.S., and take your pet along! I do not recommend leaving your pet for any length of time, but you could get in a few runs each day and come home to play with Rover in the snow... The folks at Topnotch are really dog-friendly!

Hotels/Motels
Topnotch Resort and Spa
Mountain Road
Stowe, VT 05672
(802) 253-8585

Festivals/Happenings

Mozart & Folk Art / Flower Festival (June/July)
There's always something happening in the summer near the Green Mountain Inn built in 1833. The inn itself offers "Attraction" and "Romance" packages which include all the festivities and dinner, but the town of Stowe is lovely and peaceful. And the SKIING! Don't miss the Shelburne Museum in Burlington--a lovely outside restoration of typical Vermont village (a delight) that you can walk your leashed pooch through. Vermonters are pretty good about dogs; it's a nice place to travel with your pooch.

Hotels/Motels

The Green Mountain Inn	Amenities: R,SK	Cost: ***

Main Street
P.O. Box 60
Stowe, VT 05672
(802) 253-7301

Craftsbury Antiques and Uniques
A lovely inn that accepts big dogs is a great thing to find, and there's one here. It also has a pool, tennis, and a relaxing garden for patrons to enjoy. Craftsbury hosts the summer festival, **Antiques and Uniques**, in July. The rest of the year you can find sculling, rowing, canoeing, cross-country skiing and other sports at the Craftsbury Sports Center.

Close to Stowe and downhill skiing in the winter, the inn makes a wonderful winter retreat.

The Inn On the Common   Amenities:R   Cost:**
Craftsbury, VT
(802) 586-9619

Camp Gone To The Dogs

Swimming lessons for your dog, square dancing with pet, tail-wagging competitions, costume parade, frisbee catching, tracking and obedience classes (if you need them) are all part of the fun at Camp Gone To The Dogs. Honey Loring, the owner, told me that she is booked solid months in advance so you'd better hurry and get in your reservation for next year!

Camp Gone To The Dogs
Putney School
Putney, VT
(802) 387-5673

Hikes

Appalachian Trail /Stafford
(Note: I did 20 miles of this section at age 15; it was a killer.)
Bald Mountain Trail/Townshend State Forest
Jay Peak/Westfield
Grout Pond Trail/Green Mountain Nat'l. Forest
South Trail/Willoughby State Forest
Stevenson Brook Trail/Little River State Park

Selected Covered Bridges

Columbia Bridge/Lemington
Cornish-Windsor Bridge/Windsor
Creamery Bridge/Brattleboro
Lincoln Bridge/Woodstock
Northfield Falls Bridge/Northfield
Paper Mill Bridge/Bennington
Middle Bridge/Woodstock

NORTHEAST

Pulp Mill Bridge/Middlebury
Silk Bridge/Bennington
Comstock Bridge/Montgomery

Scenic Drives
Smugglers Notch Highway - Follow State Route 108 from Stowe to
Cambridge and pass through Smugglers Notch with its beautiful
scenery and wonderful rare plant life.

Bennington Road Cut - In Woodford there is a setting that illustrates
geologic formations well and has several different and unique
harvestable rocks.

Middlebury Gap - Head to Ripton, the former home of Robert Frost
(see also New Hampshire) and pass through the famed Green
Mountains, near Middlebury College. From East Middlebury right to
the Gap.

NORTHEAST

MID-ATLANTIC

MID-ATLANTIC

Delaware
District of Columbia
Maryland
New Jersey
Pennsylvania
Virginia
West Virginia

Hotel Cost Codes (for average one-night stay)

*	$30-60/night
**	$61-100/night
***	$101-150/night
****	$151 and up/night
W	Hotel has weekly rates only

Note: costs may vary by season.

Hotel Amenity Codes

A	Airport nearby
H	Handicapped access
HS	Hair salon on premises
G	Golf within 10 miles
NS	Non-smoking rooms available
OB	Facility is on the beach
P	Playground on premises
R	Restaurant on premises
S	Swimming on premises
SA	Sauna on premises
SK	Skiing within 25 miles
T	Tennis within 10 miles

MID-ATLANTIC

MID-ATLANTIC
Delaware

Sights/Towns To See

Wilmington

The Brandywine Valley seems particularly pet-friendly, with a number of fun events. The Wilmington area offers **A Day in Old New Castle** (in May) which is an event-filled afternoon during which you and your pet can visit this lovely colonial town, walk the river walkway, and sample the quaint shops. **Art on the Green**, also in New Castle, allows you and Fifi an appreciation of the finer things each September. The **Brandywine Arts Festival** is also pet-friendly, a bit more encompassing of art forms, and is held in Brandywine Park (also pet-friendly all year). Two major attractions are Winterthur and Longwood Gardens, but neither is pet friendly, so you must go alone and leave your friend at the hotel (if allowed).

Hotels/Motels

Best Western Brandywine Valley Inn   Amenities: N/A   Cost**
1807 Concord Pike
Wilmington, DE 19803
(302) 656-9436

Econo Lodge   Amenities: N/A   Cost**
232 S. Dupont Hwy.
New Castle, DE 19702
(302) 322-4500

Arden

The entire village is in the National Register of historic places! Cute enclaves and homes of artisans and craftspeople are there for your entertainment. No one actually owns his or her home though! The village developed a 99-year lease program where your rent is your local tax!

Christiana

An important intersection during the Revolutionary War, troops made their way through Christiana from both north and south. Many of the homes are on the National Register and I'm sure you'll find at least one "George Washington slept here" scribbled on a bedpost in town.

Delaware Tourism
(302) 739-4271

Lewes

Accessible from Cape May, New Jersey, Lewes is the oldest settlement in Delaware. Visit the University of Delaware's College of Marine Studies on **Coast Day** in the fall, or stop at the DeVries Monument commemorating the 1631 settlement.

Lewes Chamber of Commerce
(302) 645-8073

Lewes Historical Complex
(302) 645-7670

Festivals/Happenings

The Sea Witch Festival (October)
Rehobeth Beach
A Fiddler's convention, laser show, Best Costumed Pet Competition, beach equestrian show, and fun games like the Pumpkin Roll entertain all who come to this festival. Costumed residents and clerks delight visitors with clues left in local stores for the unusual Sea Witch Hunt.

Sea Witch Festival
(800) 441-1329

Dog Friendly Beaches
Cape Henlopen State Park
North Fenwick Island State Park/ Select beaches
All areas labeled for fishing

MID-ATLANTIC

District of Columbia

Sights/Towns To See
The Mall
The largest piece of happy dog grassy knoll for miles around, and host to a myriad of wonderful sites including the various parts of the Smithsonian museum, the Capitol building, the White House, the lovely Reflecting Pool (seen in so many shots of the Mall; e.g."Forest Gump"), the Washington Monument, and a fun rhinoceros sculpture. If you've never been to our nation's Capitol, I suggest the **Cherry Blossom Festival** (April) or a **4th of July** visit.

It's amazing to see the masses of people gather to celebrate the birth of our nation. The music is varied depending where you sit, but you can find everything from classical to rock and every type of individual (especially fun if you're a people watcher like me!). I like to sit on the Capitol steps for a good view of one of the best fireworks displays in the U.S. Strangers become friends when the fireworks begin, and it is marvelous to experience.

Two caveats: First, it gets awful hot for your pooch so bring lots of water. Secondly, make sure your dog doesn't mind loud noises. Many dogs <u>do</u> mind loud noises, and it is a very painful experience for them. Think about protecting their hearing either by leaving the Mall just before the fireworks and watching them from any of the other great locations in and around DC or watching from your hotel.

Festivals/Happenings
March For The Animals/World Congress for Animals (June)
Hear internationally recognized speakers such as Jane Goodall and Carl Sagan, see fabulous exhibits, enjoy the vegetarian feast and gala, etc. Run Fido on the Mall (see above).
"March"
The Humane Society of the United States (HSUS)
2100 L Street NW
Washington, DC 20037
(202) 452-1100

MID-ATLANTIC

Festival of American Folk Life (July)
A wonderful 3-5 day festival crafts, music and art on The Mall. Dancing, ethnic crafts from different sections of the U.S., theater and music fill this event with excitement.

The Smithsonian
(202) 357-2700

Folk Life Festival
(202) 357-4574

Annual Bark Ball (June-first week)
Hosted by Honorary chairdogs the likes of Millie "Bush", Breezy "Quayle", Spike "Rivers" and other pooches of famous dog lovers, this ball is the place to have fun. Held in the Grand Ballroom of the Loews L'Enfant Plaza, gala attendees are formally attired in black ties and snazzy dresses (the canine attendees, that is---but we hope you dress at least as well as your pooch!) A great vegetarian buffet is served to all and there is a bar for the dogs. Attendants will take your dog outside if a pressing need arises. Heaven. Dinner, dancing, great food and my happy dog. BowWow.
Diana Kaiser
Chairperson
(202) 646-4436

Hotels/Motels
Loews L'Enfant Plaza   Amenities: R   Cost:***
480 L'Enfant Plaza SW
Washington, D.C.
(202) 484-1000

The Four Seasons   Amenities: R   Cost:***
2800 Pennsylvania Ave. NW
Washington, DC
(202) 342-0444

MID-ATLANTIC

Maryland

Sights/Towns To See

Annapolis Naval Academy
Annapolis is on the water and a very walkable city; the historic district is only about a half mile in diameter and pets are welcome at the visitor center where they will help you find pet-friendly activities. Great restaurants and shops abound in this historic district.

The Naval Academy is a wonderful site to see beautiful buildings and inscriptions about famous alumni. Lovely walks near the ocean are the order of the day here. I hope you'll get a chance somehow, by either walking by the choir office or near the chapel, to hear the wonderful Navy hymn whose words are inscribed overhead in a commemorative plaque. "Eternal Father strong to save..."

Visitor's Center
(410) 268-7676
Naval Academy Visitors Center
(410) 293-3363

Hotels/Motels
Loews Hotel   Amenities: N/A   Cost: ***
126 West Street
Annapolis, MD 21401
(410) 263-7777

Linganore Wine Cellars/ Berrywine Plantations
This dog-friendly vineyard allows you to picnic with Fido anytime, but also sponsors great festivals for you and your best friend. The **Strawberry Wine Festival** and the **Blueberry Wine Festival** feature local berry wines for sipping, and at least two different bands (Rock or Easy listening) for your aural entertainment. Other festivals throughout the year include a **Reggae Festival** featuring Caribbean food and either ginger mead or raspberry wine, and a **Bayou-Razz Jazz Festival** with

a New Orleans theme (catered by Copeland Restaurant). Located in
Mt. Airy, 4 miles off I-70; take exit 62 to New Market.

Linganore Wine Cellars
(301) 831-5889

Hotels/Motels
Comfort Inn   Amenities: H,R,SK   Cost: **
420 Prospect Blvd.
Frederick, MD 21701
(301) 695-6200

Holiday Inn Express   Amenities: R,SK   Cost: **
5579 Spectrum Drive
Frederick, MD 21701
(301) 695-2881

Tangier Island Cruises
Explore Tangier Island with a pet-friendly cruise from Crisfeld.
Fishing is almost exclusively the island's only way to make a living.
They have an unusually British accent for folks who broke away from
Britain in 1776. It is a relaxing island cruise for you and the hound.

Tangier Island Cruises
Crisfeld, MD
(410) 968-2338

Festivals/Happenings
Salute to Elvis Presley (August)
Fell's Point Square (Baltimore City)
This is a yearly tribute to the King complete with impersonators, Elvis
memorabilia on display and available for purchase, and live music.
Credo Elvem ipsum etiam vivere! [Elvis lives!] Be a part of the
festivities and enter the look-alike or the "Let Me Be Your Teddy
Bear" contest. They welcome your pooch and, who knows, maybe
they'll listen to your version of "Hound Dog" in one of the contests!
At the Marriott and the Glen Burnie you can SAVE 50% on your room
(see Pet Care Savings Club in appendix)!

MID-ATLANTIC

Elvis Salute
(410) 396-9177

Hotels/Motels
Baltimore Marriott Inner Harbor   Amenities: R,T   Cost:***
Pratt & Eutaw St.
Baltimore, MD
(410) 962-0202
(800) 228-9290

Glen Burnie Holiday Inn   Amenities: R,T   Cost:***
6323 Richie Hwy.
Glen Burnie, MD
(410) 636-4300

Jackson Marine Boat Show and Flea Market (August)
North East (Exit 100 off I-95)
Largest display of used and brokerage boats in the area. Marine store
sale, flea market, free refreshments, and door prizes. You and your pet
can check out the right watercraft for the two of you. Whatever floats
your boat!

Jackson Marine Sales
(410) 287-9400

Big Band Night (August)
St. Michaels
At the Chesapeake Bay Maritime Museum every summer. Live band
delights the crowd with dinner dance music from the 30's and 40's.
Bring an elaborate picnic dinner (wine, cheese, breads, etc.) and dine
and dance under the stars with your pet. Well, dancing might be
problematic. OK, dine with Fido and dance by yourself or with a
member of the species *Homo sapiens* (or at least someone in the
mammal category). "A loaf of bread, a jug of wine, and thou, Fido,
beside me..."

Chesapeake Bay Maritime Museum
(410) 745-2916

MID-ATLANTIC

Sugarloaf Art Fair (November)
Gaithersburg
A gathering of 300 to 500 of the finest artists and crafts designers on the East Coast. There are different locations around the country. Maryland and Virginia are the only outdoor venues though, and your pet is tacitly allowed in a sort of "don't-bark-don't-tell" policy. [PAY HALF PRICE at Econo Lodge! See appendix.]

Hotels/Motels
Econo Lodge   Amenities:N/A   Cost:**
18715 N. Frederick Ave.
Gaithersburg, MD
(301) 963-3840

PAW Pet Photo Day/Doggie Fun Day (September)
Germantown/Laurel
Doggie Fun Day takes place at the Cherry Lane Kennels, where there will be lots of dog-related products and activities. Pet Photo Day occurs at the Petsmart, where numerous pet products can be found as well.

PAW (Partnership for Animal Welfare)
(800) 654-6825
(301) 340-0652

Dog Friendly Beaches
Ocean City
Assateague Island

New Jersey

Sights/Towns To See

Chester/Mendham
A charming area where dogs are welcome just about everywhere. Nearly everyone has a pet of some kind. Check out the more than 60 adorable shops in the peaceful town of Chester. The kids and pooch on a leash will enjoy the menagerie of exotic and farm animals at Larison's Turkey Farm. Stop in at Aunt Pittypat's and find great antiques and reproduction furniture. Pegasus Antiques (too crowded for pets), on the corner across from the Public House Inn and restaurant, has the most incredible mish-mash of geegaws I have ever seen! There is a new Emack & Bolio's Ice Cream Parlor in the heart of Mendham across from the ever-popular Black Horse Tavern, and the Dairy Queen in Chester regularly gives out little dog cones. At the Peapack-Gladstone Bank, they always have dog biscuits at the ready and give them out to each dog customer. Need to let the dog run? There are 3 parks in Chester where your pooch will be happy.

Hotels/Motels
The Inn at Millrace Pond   Amenities: N/A   Cost: ***
P.O. Box 359
Hope, NJ 07844
(908) 459-4884

Howard Johnson Lodge   Amenities: H,R,S,NS   Cost: ***
Green Pond Road
Rockaway, NJ 07866
(201) 625-1200

Cape May
A beautiful coastline, lovely victorian homes and clever little shops make Cape May an ideal destination for families with pets. There's lots to see while walking around and you can take turns holding Fido outside the shops that will not let him come in. Three beaches are available to you and your pet, Higbee Beach, Diamond Beach and

Cape May Point. You can bird or look for shells or interesting detritus in the rocks while Fido runs in the surf. There is only one hotel in Cape May proper that accepts pets all summer, the Marquis de Lafayette. While it has an ideal location on the beach, this means that you must book well in advance to assure a place. There are other hotels nearby, though. Cape May plays host to several festivals throughout the year, like Victorian Christmas tours and Sherlock Holmes Mystery weekends in the fall.

Hotels/Motels

Marquis de Lafayette   Amenities: OB   Cost: ***
501 Beach Drive
Cape May, NJ 08204
(800) 257-0432
(609) 884-3500

Cabin City Motel   Amenities: N/A   Cost: **
756 Route 9
Cape May, NJ 08204
(609) 884-8551

Long Beach Lounge   Amenities: S,OB   Cost: **
539 East 9th Ave.
North Wildwood, NJ 08260
(609) 522-1520

New England Motel   Amenities: N/A   Cost: **
106 West 11th Street
North Wildwood, NJ 08260
(609) 522-7250

Woodbury Motel/Apts.   Amenities: H,G,T   Cost: **
407 Surf Ave.
North Wildwood, NJ 08260
(609) 522-7315

MID-ATLANTIC

Festivals/Happenings
Festival By The Bay (June)
Crafters, live entertainment, historical and environmental exhibits, demonstrations and food, fun and games can be found in this park by the sea. Marina Park allows your pet all the time as well as at this festival.

42nd St. and The Bay
Sea Isle City
(609) 263-6200

Bergen County Outdoor Art Show & Concert (June)
Juried fine arts show in Van Saun County Park. Award categories for you to judge as well as an afternoon concert. Pets on 6 ft. leash welcome in the park and the festival.

Bergen County Art Show
Van Saun Park
Forest and Continental Ave.
(201) 646-2780

Table Settings and Garden Boutique (June)
Martha Stewart would be proud. A dog lover herself, she'd appreciate being invited to the finer festivals avec pooch. This is a showcase of lovely table settings and ideas for entertaining. An outdoor boutique allows you to share the wealth of the gardens of this lovely estate, The Hermitage. It is expected that you will keep Fido under control. Near Ridgewood in Bergen county, this estate is easy to get to off Rte. 287.

Table Settings and Garden Boutique
The Hermitage
335 North Franklin Turnpike
Ho-Ho-Kus, NJ
(201) 445-8311

Movies Under the Stars (June/July)
Bring your blanket, picnic dinner, lawn chair, and a happy dog to this outdoor film festival. It is held every Thursday night during the summer at the Erie Lackawanna Plaza in front of the train station.

MID-ATLANTIC

There are live concerts (Jazz, Big Band, Rock, Swing, etc.) in Church Square Park at 4th and Garden St. every Wednesday evening as well. The park is nearby and there is a dog run.

Movies Under the Stars
1 Hudson Place
Hoboken, NJ
(201) 420-2207

Our Loveladies Fair
Long Beach Island is home to many artists and clever crafters and this is the first introduction of the summer for visitors. Many other merchants also display their wares. Both mainland and island merchants are present. Pets are, of course, allowed.

Our Loveladies Fair
120 Long Beach Boulevard
Loveladies, NJ
(609) 494-1241

Annual Somerville Street Festival
Live entertainment, craft vendors, children's activities and international foods. Somerville has an abundance of wonderful ethnic restaurants from Japanese to Spanish to Indian.

Main Street
Somerville, NJ
(908) 526-3499
(908) 996-3036

American Spaniel Club (January)
Meadowlands Hilton
Secaucus, NJ
(706) 860-0881

St. Hubert's Giralda Dog Walk and Fair (May)
An annual festival of dogs, to benefit one of the country's best animal shelters. Hundreds of canines and their owners participate in this walkathon and fair. There are dog products, sponsor competitions,

Do-you-look-like-your-dog? competitions, games, lure coursing, and all kinds of contests, music and fun food.
Giralda Farms
Route 124
Madison, NJ
(201) 514-5888

The Essex Horse Trials (March)
USET Facility
Gladstone, NJ
(908) 234-1251

Pet Fair
Displays, demonstrations, pet portraits, adoption, frisbee dogs, sled dogs, etc.
Trailside Nature & Science Center
Mountainside, NJ
452 New Providence Rd.
(908) 789-3670

Far Hills Race Meeting (October)
An exciting event with perpetual tailgating, exotic foods, wild spectators and beautiful horses in a dangerous sport.
AT&T Moorland Farms
Far Hills, NJ
(908) 685-2929

Hotels/Motels
The Inn at Millrace Pond   Amenities: N/A   Cost: ***
P.O. Box 359
Hope, NJ 07844
(908) 459-4884

Howard Johnson Lodge   Amenities: H,R,S,NS   Cost: ***
Green Pond Road
Rockaway, NJ 07866
(201) 625-1200

MID-ATLANTIC

Days Inn   Amenities: H,R,G,NS   Cost: ***
3159 Rt. 46
Parsippany, NJ 07054
(201) 335-0200

Dog Friendly Beaches
Cape May/Higbee Beach
Cape May/Cape May Point
Cape May/Diamond Beach
Sandy Hook National Recreation Area
Lakewood/ South Lake Drive (across from the college)
Lakewood/ Ocean County Park (Route 88)

Pennsylvania

Sights/Towns To See

Lancaster

You're in Pennsylvania Dutch Country and the pace is nice and easy. Black horse-drawn buggies are ubiquitous in Lancaster as the Amish drive to the beat of their own drummer. Antiques, folk art, crafts, quilts and those Amish hex signs are available everywhere.

In the mood for food? There is a smorgasbord here. Although it's the Licorice capital of the world, Lancaster has much more to offer than confections, although there's a lot of sugar here. The Wilbur Chocolate Factory in Lititz sends out chemical messages in the form of chocolate odors that assault all who pass by. What a way to go! Nearby Hershey has the largest chocolate factory in the world as well as lamps that look like Hershey's Kisses and people dressed as chocolate snacks running all around town.

Many pretzel factories are within a short distance (Herr's Snack Factory in Nottingham, Anderson Pretzel Bakery in Lancaster etc.). The Sturgis Pretzel House, in operation since the 1700's, teaches you how to make your own pretzels. (Dogs are prohibited from food establishments, but you can bring him/her home some pretzels!) Did you know that low-fat (most of them are), low-salt hard pretzels are GOOD for both you and your dog?!! They not only supply carbohydrates, but a necessary teeth-cleaning action that keeps and your gums (and your dog's!) healthy and pink.

The General Sutter Inn   Amenities:N/A   Cost:***
14 East Main St.
Lititz, PA 17543
(717) 626-2115

Holiday Inn   Amenities: R   Cost:**
Route 441 & I-283 (4751 Lindle Rd.)
Harrisburg, PA 17111
(800) 637-4817

Sturgis Pretzel House
East Main St.
Lititz, PA 17543
(717) 626-4354

York
Old fashioned gaslights and cobblestone streets lead you to dozens of
lovely little shops, art galleries, and reataurants in this town that, in
1777, proclaimed the first National Thanksgiving Day.   Home to
several important historical buildings such as the Courthouse where the
First Continental Congress met when the British occupied Philadelphia,
one might not expect to find that one of the main attractions here is
quite modern.   Walk the cute streets of town with the hound and you'll
find, not the Weightlifting Hall of Fame (although that is here too!), but
the Harley-Davidson motorcycle plant! Yup, you're in Hawg Heaven!
There is a museum here that has the first Harley ever made along with
models from each successive year so you can trace their development.
Not into bikes? Well, the pooch can't go into the plant or museum
anyway, so just take a long stroll and enjoy the whole atmosphere.

The York Chamber of Commerce
(800) 673-2429

Punxatawney
Will it be another six months of winter?   Only Punxatawney Phil
knows for sure.   Each year on February second, Punxatawney
celebrates Ground Hog Day along with ten thousand invited guests.
It's a lot of fun; a regular eating and drinking fest.   But my favorite
aspect to this adventure is the fact that one of my all-time favorite
movies was all about this winter day in a small town in Pennsylvania;
"Ground Hog Day" with Andie MacDowell and Bill Murray.   If you
haven't seen it, rent it.   If you're visiting here, rent it.   It's not what
you'd expect...Oh, and keep your dog on a leash; you don't want any
dog-hog interactions.

Punxatawney Chamber of Commerce
(814) 938-7700

Country Villa Route 119 South Punxatawney, PA 15767 (814) 938-8330	Amenities:N/A	Cost:***
HoJo Inn 245 Allegheny Blvd. Brookville, PA 15825 (814) 849-3335	Amenities: R,NS	Cost: *
Ramada Limited 235 Allegheny Blvd. Brookville, PA 15825 (814) 849-8381	Amenities:G,R,S,NS	Cost:*
Pantall Hotel 135 E. Mahoning St. Punxsatawney, PA 15767 (814) 938-6600	Amenities: N/A	Cost:**

Gettysburg
Dogs on leash are welcomed at this site of one of the turning points of the Civil War. A Union victory here stopped the offensive maneuvers of the Confederacy and sent them into retreat. It was the beginning of the fall of the South, and there was a great loss of life for the cause. Abraham Lincoln gave his famous address after the battle here in 1863, "Fourscore and seven years ago our fathers brought forth on this continent a new nation, conceived in liberty, and dedicated to the proposition that all men are created equal....Now we are engaged in a great civil war, testing whether that nation....can long endure. ...We here highly resolve that these dead shall not have died in vain; that this new nation, under God, shall have a new birth of freedom; and government of the people, by the people, for the people, shall not perish from the earth." A great moment in history. Relive it.

MID-ATLANTIC

There is a driving tour of 18 miles that Fido will enjoy as well as hikes through various parts of the park; the Billy Yank or Johnny Reb Trail, or the Mile High Water Mark Trail that still has artillery remnants on the field. Many museums and shops are located nearby (some allow pets) and you can pick up a souvenir or two.

Gettysburg Travel Council
(717) 334-6274

Holiday Inn Battlefield   Amenities: N/A   Cost:**
516 Baltimore St.
Gettysburg, PA 17325
(717) 334-6211

Howard Johnson Lodge   Amenities: N/A   Cost:**
301 Steinwehr Ave.
Gettysburg, PA 17325
(717) 334-1188

The Poconos
Skiing, hiking, golfing, tennis, water sports, headliner acts, comedy and romantic getaways can be found here. Bushkill Falls, "The Niagara of Pennsylvania", can be found here as well. It has 300 acres of pet friendly hiking, 8 cascading waterfalls, picnic areas, and lots of fudge, ice cream and miniature golf. The Glenwood offers "the best Dog-Gone vacation around", and they mean it. You can bring your small dog and have access to a myriad of free activities from all the above plus bocce to nightly dancing and revelry.

Ski areas include Alpine Mt. in Analomink, Shawnee and Camelback near Tannersville, Jack Frost and Big Boulder near Lake Harmony in the west Poconos, and Tanglewood in the west. Most of them are less than an hour apart in any direction. Alpine, Shawnee and Camelback are near Stroudsberg.

Pocono Chamber Of Commerce
(800) POCONOS

MID-ATLANTIC

Bushkill Falls
Route 209
Bushkill, PA 18324
(717) 588-6682

Colony Motor Lodge   Amenities: G,T,SK Cost:**
1863 W, Main St.
Stroudsberg, PA
(717) 421-3790

Budget Motor Lodge   Amenities: G,T,SK Cost:**
I-80 Exit 51
East Stroudsberg, PA 18301
(800) 233-8144

Glenwood Resort   Amenities:G,T,SK   Cost:**
Main St., P.O. Box 159
Delaware Water Gap, PA 18327
(800) 833-3050
(717) 476-0010

Best Western Inn   Amenities:G,T,SK,R   Cost: **
900 Routes 6 & 209
Matamoras, PA 18336
(717) 491-2400
(800) 528-1234

Mountain Laurel Resort   Amenities:G,T,SK,R   Cost: ***
I-80 at Northeast Ext.
White Haven, PA 18661
(717) 443-8411

Holiday Inn   Amenities: G,T,SK Cost:**
Bartonsville, PA
(800) 231-3321

Rimrock Cottages   Amenities: G,T,SK Cost:**
Bartonsville, PA
(717) 629-2360

MID-ATLANTIC

Alvin's Log Cabins   Amenities: G,T,SK Cost:**
Henryville, PA
(717) 629-0667

Martin's Cottages   Amenities: G,T,SK Cost:**
Hawley, PA
(717) 226-9621

Bucks County
Bucks County was an artist's haven many years ago, and today many
wonderful local artists and craftsmen still show and sell their wares in
the New Hope/ Lambertville area. Great restaurants and cute shops
abound on both sides of the Delaware River, which can be viewed as
you walk, with Fido, across the bridge that connects Pennsylvania and
New Jersey. You can find lots of outdoor cafes and dining, and after
you've seen the two towns there are several nature walks nearby--one
at the site where Washington crossed the Delaware. Check out the
antique shops and the Lambertville Flea market where great buys can
be found (both antiques and newer items).

Bucks County Horse Park
Bucks County Horse Park is a 700 acre facility with 25 miles of trails
that welcomes dogs and their owners as well as horses. There is (for
horses and owners) show jumping, carriage driving, polo, dressage, and
trail riding. Call the numbers below to receive a schedule of the many
exciting annual events.

Festivals/Happenings
Team Chase (April)
Bucks County Horse Park
Revere, PA 18953
(610) 847-8597

Polo & Pooches Dog Show (August)
Bucks County Horse Park
Revere, PA 18953
(610) 847-8597

MID-ATLANTIC

Hotels/Motels
Comfort Suites   Amenities: R,G,T,SK   Cost: **
120 W. Third St,
Bethlehem, PA 18015
(610) 882-9700

Memorial Weekend Classic/Dog Show (May)
Lawrence County Farm Show Grounds
New Castle, PA

Contact:
John Wood, Coordinator
(412) 487-8169
Lee Herr, Coordinator
(412) 758-5699

Wiz Kid Dog Camp
Dogs love it and their owners can learn something too! Lodging is
provided at the local Holiday Inn for a nominal fee.
Wiz Kid Dog Camp
Morgantown, PA

Wiz Kid Dog Camp
4 Brookside Pl.
Westport, CT 06880
(203) 226-9556

Virginia

Sights/Towns To See

Colonial Williamsburg
Always the highlight of my trip to Virginia, Colonial Williamsburg is a National Historic Landmark and was the capital city of Virginia from 1699-1780. It contains hundreds of historic and reproduction buildings, taverns, shops, formal gardens and guided tours. Your dog is welcome on a leash at any of the outdoor facilities. You can eat your picnic lunch outdoors as well. The dog is also welcome on the bus from the visitor center to the historic site (it's included in your ticket price). Although the dog cannot view the film at the visitor center, you can get yourself in the proper mood by renting one of my favorite films (in which I'm sure there are some shots of Williamsburg!), the always inspiring "1776" (with Blythe Danner and William Daniels) before you come. Don't miss Carter's Grove, a Georgian country plantation built in 1750, which is several miles outside of Williamsburg. They too welcome your pet on leash!

Colonial Williamsburg
(804) 229-1000
Carter's Grove
(804) 229-1000

Hotels/Motels
Williamsburg Woodlands   Amenities:R,S   Cost: ***
102 Visitor's Center Drive
Williamsburg, VA 23185
(804) 253-2277

Governor's Inn   Amenities:R,S   Cost:***
506 North Henry Street
Williamsburg, VA
(804) 253-2277

Berkeley
Start your tour of Southern plantations with this dog-friendly (outside only please) Georgian mansion built in 1619. Site of the first Thanksgiving, birthplace of Benjamin Harrison (he signed the Declaration of Independence), the mournful song played at important military events, "Taps", was composed on these grounds in 1862. (Six miles west of Charles City.) Dine out with your pet at the wonderful Coach House Tavern next to Berkeley. Several tables are available, some with shade and enclosed by garden flora.

Berkeley
(804) 829-6018
Coach House Tavern
(804) 829-6003

Sherwood Forest
A working plantation once owned by two different U.S. Presidents! Both William Henry Harrison and John Tyler lived in this 300 foot long house, recently declared the longest frame house in the U.S. The grounds are large and accomodating of you and your pet (on a leash) and dogs are welcomed. The inside of the house is off limits to your pet, however you may explore the historic land at your leisure. (Seven miles south of Providence Forge). Williamsburg is only 25 min.

Sherwood Forest
(804) 829-5377
Sherwood Forest Giftshop
(804) 829-9435

Smithfield
Take your pet on a walking tour of the more than 65 homes and public buildings in this lovely area. See a mix of 18th century, Georgian and Victorian homes in this pre-colonial town. Arthur Smith patented 1450 acres of land adjacent to the Pagan River in September 1637. In 1752, British merchants and sea captains settled this town, and 15 of the houses are authentic 18th century and predate the Revolutionary War.

Festivals/Happenings

Christmas in July/Pet Portraits
Smithfield
A fund raiser for the Isle of Wight Humane Society, a local
professional will take pictures of your pet with Santa. Use the result
for next year's Christmas card!

The Collage
346 Main St.
Smithfield, VA
(804) 357-7707

Dog Days Contest (August)
Smithfield
Downtown merchants provide festivities and food for the races, dog
show, and other low-key competitions for pets and purebreds. Fun for
both you and your friend.

Old Courthouse, Main Street
Contact: Lona Ellis
(757) 357-3288

Blessing of the Animals (October)
Smithfield
Blessing of the animals at St. Lukes in Smithfield on the eve of the
Feast of St. Francis. A national shrine, it is the oldest Anglican church
on American soil.

Chamber of Commerce
(800) 365-9339

Isle of Wight County Fair (September)
Smithfield
Isle of Wight's old fashioned celebration includes horseshoe contests,
steam engines, tether rides, mule pulls, rollerblade hockey (the pre-
Revolutionary version), country music, games, and food. Several
contests include everything from livestock to quilts. (Check Newport
News or Norfolk for places to stay.)

MID-ATLANTIC

Isle of Wight County Fair
(804) 357-2291

Smithfield Office of Tourism
(804) 357-5182

Four Square Plantation   Amenities: N/A   Cost:**
13357 Four Square Road
Smithfield, VA
(757) 365-0749

Fredricksburg
Annual Dog Mart (October)
Fredricksburg
That this festival has reportedly been running for over 200 years proves
that Virginia is dog-friendly.   Demonstrations,   pet products for
purchase, a low-key dog show for family pets, and many activities by
local tribes make this a one of a kind event.
(540) 972-7615

Fredricksburg Dog Festival (October)
Fredricksburg
A day of celebrating canines everywhere. A dog parade and numerous
contests punctuate this festival for man's best friend.
(703) 372-1086

Hotels/Motels
Ramada Inn   Amenities: R   Cost:**
Spotsylvania Mall
Rte. 3 West
Fredericksburg, VA 22404
(540) 786-8361

Hopewell
There are two main attractions in Hopewell; Appomatox Manor (the
dog is allowed on the grounds only) and the City Point district.   A
walking tour reveals some very interesting homes--many very nice
homes that were, in fact, ordered out of the Sears catalogue when it
sold homes in the 1920's! There is a cruise on The Pocahontas II that

allows you and your leashed pet to view all the plantations on the James River accompanied by historical narration.

The Pocahontas II
(800) 405-9990

Norfolk
How about a Mississippi Riverboat tour on a restored 19th century paddleboat? Your pet is welcome on the outer deck (food is served inside) of this exciting tour of Norfolk / Portsmouth harbor, the Naval Shipyard, warships, submarines, and aircraft carriers. Take time to look for interesting waterfowl near the boat or further out in the harbor.

Hotels/Motels
Comfort Inn   Amenities: H,R,SA   Cost: *
930 Virginia Beach Blvd.
Norfolk, VA 23504
(804) 623-5700

Econo Lodge   Amenities: G,H,R,T,SA Cost: *
9601 4th View St.
Norfolk, VA 23503
(804) 480-9611

Campsites
Note: All Virginia campsites allow leashed dogs. I have only listed a few here for your interest. There are many more.

Amelia Family Campground, Amelia	(804) 561-3011
Americamps, North Ashland	(804) 798-5298
Aquia Pines Campground, Stafford	(703) 659-3447
Cambrae Lodge KOA, Charlottesville	(804) 296-9881
Camper's Ranch, Chincoteague	(804) 336-6371
Jellystone Camp/Resort, Greenwood	(703) 456-6409
Chesapeake KOA, Chesapeake	(804) 485-5686
Colonial Campground, Williamsburg	(804) 565-2734
Davis Mobile Home, Newport News	(804) 244-5030

Scenic Drives
Blue Ridge Parkway
Drive along the top of the mountains near Waynesboro from Virginia to North Carolina and continue through the Great Smoky Mountains National Park. The whole trip is almost 500 miles at a maximum speed of 45 mph. Do a little each day as you wind through Virginia.

Skyline Drive
Right through Shenandoah National Park, this is a stunning drive complete with 600 ft. tunnel and numerous overlooks. Joins Blue Ridge Parkway in the south. (100 miles)

Route 39
If you like gorges you'll love this drive, as both sides of the road rise steeply away from you when you pass through several sections of this rugged highway. Lovely pines and evergreen bushes fill the rest of this scenic drive. (3 miles)

West Virginia

Sights/Towns To See

Wheeling
City Of Lights Festival (November-January)
Wheeling
Thousands and thousands of lights illuminate this downtown holiday festival. Victorian house tours, Fantasy in Light Parade, specialty shops and holiday opportunities can be found throughout this several week festival.

City Of Lights Festival
(304) 233-2575
(800) 828-3097

Winter Festival of Lights (November-January)
Wheeling/Oglebay Park
Miles of huge light displays highlighting that you and your pet can drive through. Architectural and landscape lighting provide this 300 acre park with a real holiday glow. Guided tour or drive through on your own.

Festival of Lights
(304) 243-4032
(800) 624-6988

Upper Ohio Valley Italian Festival (July)
Wheeling
Three stages full of entertainment in downtown Wheeling support this days-long continuous festival. Strolling minstrels, and boccie and morra tournaments supplement wonderful ethnic foods and crafts. Your pet is welcome.

Italian Festival
(304) 828-3097

Hotels/Motels
Comfort Inn   Amenities: G,T,R,S   Cost: *
I-70
Wheeling, WV
(304) 547-1380

Days Inn   Amenities: G,T,R,S   Cost: *
I-70
Wheeling, WV
(304) 547-0610

Festivals/Happenings

Thunder in the Mountains/ Racing and Auto Show (May)
Mineral Wells/4-H grounds
NASCAR drivers and cars, hot rod and antique cars drive this benefit event. (pardon the pun). This is a family show with live entertainment, fireworks and an auction. The dog is welcome. Great fun if you're into hot cars.

Thunder in the Mountains
(304) 295-6139

Hotels/Motels
Comfort Inn   Amenities:G,T,R,S   Cost: *
I-70
Wheeling, WV 26059
(304) 547-1380

Days Inn   Amenities: G,T,R,S   Cost: *
I-70
Wheeling, WV 26059
(304) 547-0610

Oglebay Resort   Amenities: G,T,H,R,S   Cost: **
Route 88N
Wheeling WV 26003
(800) 624-6988 (cabins only)

Oil and Gas Festival (September)
Sistersville
See the antique engines that helped the Gay Nineties flourish in the US.
Canoe races, ferryboat rides, food and good fun fuel this event with
combustive excitement. Quick, what movie did this line come from:
"Howard, you're the largest pocket of untapped natural gas known to
man..." ? [A free copy of "Take Your Pet Along" to the first 10 people
who mail the correct answer (ends October 1997) to MCE, P.O. Box
84, Chester, NJ 07930]
Oil and Gas Festival
(304) 652-2939

Hotels/Motels
The Hotel at the Wells Inn   Amenities: G,T,R   Cost: *
316 Charles St.
Sistersville, WV 26175
(304) 652-1312

Oglebay Resort   Amenities: G,T,H,R,S Cost: *
Route 88N
Wheeling WV 26003
(800) 624-6988 (cabins only)

Annual Reindog Parade (December)
Capitol Street
Charleston Festival Commission
Charleston, WV
(304) 348-6419 or (304) 346-6792

Hotels/Motels
Ramada Inn   Amenities: A,H,R,S,NS   Cost: *
2nd Ave. & B Street
Charleston, WV 25303
(304) 744-4641

Good walks (800) CALL-WVA
Kanawha State Forest /Charleston
Canaan Valley Resort State Park/Davis
Blackwater Falls/Davis

MID-ATLANTIC

SOUTHEAST

SOUTHEAST

SOUTHEAST

SOUTHEAST

Alabama
Florida
Georgia
Mississippi
North Carolina
South Carolina
Tennessee

Hotel Cost Codes (for average one-night stay)

*	$30-60/night
**	$61-100/night
***	$101-150/night
****	$151 and up/night
W	Hotel has weekly rates only

Note: costs may vary by season.

Hotel Amenity Codes

A	Airport nearby
H	Handicapped access
HS	Hair salon on premises
G	Golf within 10 miles
NS	Non-smoking rooms available
OB	Facility is on the beach
P	Playground on premises
R	Restaurant on premises
S	Swimming on premises
SA	Sauna on premises
SK	Skiing within 25 miles
T	Tennis within 10 miles

SOUTHEAST

SOUTHEAST
Alabama

Sights/Towns To See

Dauphin Island
Visit the Fort Gaines battlefields and Civil War site. Pets on leash are welcome. There are fewer people here than at many other beach attractions listed in this guide, so if it's solitude and peace you seek this is the place. There are other attractions besides the usual water sports, like the Indian Mounds, but this is no night-life hot spot.

Hotels/Motels
Gulf Breeze Motel   Amenities:N/A   Cost:**
1512 Cadillac Ave.
Dauphin Island, AL 36528
(205) 861-7344

Bessemer Flea Market (Summer)
All weekend long with 300+ booths outside where pets are welcome to walk, but they ask that you scoop (like all public places). New, old and collectible merchandise is for sale both outside and in. There are food and beverage vendors there as well--make sure your pet has shade every so often and buy him/her a beverage if no water is available. My dog likes OJ or other sweet juices (in a pinch). Dogs aren't big fans of carbonation in drinks, so be sure and get him something he'll like to drink.

Bessemer Flea Market
(205) 425-8510

Hotels/Motels
Best Western Bessemer Inn   Amenities: H,R   Cost: *
1098 Ninth Avenue SW
Bessemer, AL 35021
(800) 528-1234

DeSoto Caverns Park
Childersburg

What is larger than a football field and higher than a 12 story building? Thinking about the largest snowpile you had last winter? Well, don't. The answer is Great Onyx Cathedral at DeSoto Caverns Park, the friendliest theme park I have encountered yet. As I look at this amazing sight I wonder what it must have been like for the first person (or non-person--lets be P.C. here...) who discovered the cathedral. Movie set, gunpowder mining center, speakeasy during Prohibition, and shelter for early Indian trades; this onyx wonder was one of the first recorded caves in the U.S. Named for Hernando DeSoto who visited the area in the 1540's, this cave offers more to do than most amusement parks. Pan for gold or gemstones, see the spectacular laser show, navigate the 3/4 acre maze or just admire the natural beauty.

DeSoto Caverns Park
5181 DeSoto Caverns Pkwy.
Childersburg, AL 35044
(205) 378-7252
(800) 933-2283

Vulcan: The Iron Man
Birmingham

What's this you ask? Another Star Trek sequel? No, atop Red Mountain stands the largest cast metal sculpture in the world, Vulcan. He was supposed to be 56 ft. tall, but someone put his arm on backwards so he's only 53.6 ft. Still the world's largest. Pets are allowed to view the sculpture in the park, but may not attend the slide show about the 15 part construction and history of Vulcan. It is worth it just to see the man himself, though.

Birmingham Historical Society
(205) 251-1880

Hotels/Motels

| Comfort Inn | Amenities: G,H,R,T | Cost: ** |

4627 US 280 S.
Birmingham, AL 35242
(205) 991-9977

Festivals/Happenings

World's Largest Peanut Boil
Luverne
Give a little of your time to this Shriner's effort for the crippled and burned children of the world. Go and have a heapin' helpin' of their hospitality and enjoy the peanuts donated by the farmers of Crenshaw County. Nicest bunch of folks you'd ever want to meet. Bring your well behaved dog. Contact Aubrey Alford.

Peanut Boil
Luverne, AL
(334) 335-5516

Sand Mountain Potato Festival (June)
Henager
Parade, car show, community picnic, music, games, crafts, and the biggest fireworks display in Alabama and just about anything else you can think of that would make this sort of event special. Henager was the potato capital of the South for a long time. French fries, gater taters, ribbon and baked potatoes along with 1200 pounds of Boston butt (a curious cut of pork) and a voice from the bandstand beckon you to bake in the glow of a warm common tater.

Potato Festival
(205) 657-5849

Hotels/Motels
Econo Lodge   Amenities: N/A   Cost: *
507 Cherry Street
P.O. Box 571
Gadsden, AL 35954
(205) 538-9925

W.C. Handy Music Festival
Florence
Amazing outdoor festival with music in several towns and at least three counties, your pet will enjoy this retrospective in tribute to the "Father of the Blues", W.C. Handy.   OK, so maybe the dog doesn't care--but

he'd prefer it to a heavy metal concert! Over 100 events take place in the week long festival, including the 5K Da Doo Run Run (you gotta love it!) and the Century bike ride on the Natchez Trace Parkway.

Handy Music Festival
(205) 766-7642

Hotels/Motels
Comfort Inn   Amenities: G,H,R,T   Cost: *
400 S. Court St.
Florence, AL 35630
(205) 760-8888

Juneteenth Celebration (June)
Pritchard
Renaissance Park holds this celebration in honor of the June 1865 date that slaves in the South were notified of the 1863 signing of the Emancipation Proclamation. (I know the mail was slow then, but <u>two years</u> seems like an awfully long time to have to wait to receive such important news, doesn't it?!) Motivational speakers, great food, and lots of entertainment draw thousands of people to Pritchard in June. Pets are welcome-according to the organizer of the festival.

Juneteenth Celebration
(334) 452-6525

Jay Grelens's Sweet Tea Sip-Off
Mobile
Held at the Mobile Center every summer, this is a true Southern traditional tea, not English afternoon tea. Enter your sweet tea or teacake recipe and compete for prizes. Enjoy Southern hospitality, great tea and accompaniments even if you don't enter. And most fun of all, Fido can be by your side throughout the croquet, horsehoes and family fun.

Sweet Tea Sip-Off
(334) 973-2217
(334) 661-7647

SOUTHEAST

Hotels/Motels
Ramada Inn on the Bay   Amenities: S,H,G,T   Cost:**
Battleship Pkwy.
P.O. Box 1626
Mobile, AL 36633
(205) 626-7200

Dog Friendly Beaches
Dauphin Island

Florida

Sights/Towns To See

Disney World

A spectacular array of goings on includes Epcot center, Disney World, and now the Disney Institute (where you can apply yourself to hands-on-projects or take a class in the making of animated film, etc.).

While Disney World does not allow dogs on its grounds, it provides air-conditioned day kennels right outside the gates for patrons with dogs for $6/day. If you are staying overnight in one of Disney's resorts, the overnight kenneling cost is $11/night. There are strict rules for kenneling besides the obvious vaccinations; owners must visit their dogs and provide food and or water at least once per day. It's a reasonable compromise, but not as good as having your pet with you; on second thought, does your pet really want to ride Space Mountain?

If you don't want to kennel your pet at the theme park, the Holiday Inn in Kissimmee (3 miles from Disney World) features a Pets Are Welcome (PAW) program to deliver first-class treatment to your pet.

And for the true animal enthusiast, the Lorelei Resort near St. Petersburg caters to pets - and I mean all kinds of pets!

Hotels/Motels

Holiday Inn East-Main Gate   Amenities: R   Cost:***
5678 W. Irlo Bronson Memorial Hwy
Kissimmee, FL 34746
(407) 396-4488

Lorelei Resort   Amenities: S Cost: **
10273 Gulf Blvd.
Treasure Island, FL 33706
(800) 354-6364
(813) 360-4351

Ocala National Forest

Home to wonderful birding, hiking and just observing nature, Ocala Forest is not to be missed. Almost 500,000 acres contain hundreds of lakes and magnificent flora and fauna including some endangered species. Keep your pet on a leash and there'll be no bear-dog interactions.

Ocala National Forest
17147 E. Hwy 40
Silver Springs, FL 32688
(904) 625-7470

Sanibel Island

Peaceful, shell covered Sanibel island is the ideal destination for those of you who don't seek the wild nightlife and hot clubs of a Miami vacation. There is a wildlife preserve that covers a good deal of this little island and dogs are allowed on most public beaches. Tennis, boating and golf are favored pastimes here.

Carribe Beach Resort   Amenities:G,T   Cost:***
2669 W. Gulf Dr.
P.O. Box 158
Sanibel Island, FL 33957
(813) 472-1166
(800) 237-7370

Signal Beach & Club   Amenities:G,T   Cost:***
1811 Olde Middle Gulf Dr.
Sanibel Island, FL 33957
(813) 472-4690

Mitchell's Sand Castles   Amenities:G,T   Cost:***
3951 W. Gulf Dr.
Sanibel Island, FL 33957
(813) 472-1282

SOUTHEAST

Sarasota/ Siesta Key
Awards for the Whitest Sand Beach in the world regularly go to Turtle
Beach on Siesta Key. Dogs may only go below the high water line on
the beach and need to access it via private land. Interesting beach
rules, but important so that Fido can swim, but the beach also retains its
whiteness. Siesta Key is an 8 mile long island off the Florida coast and
considered part of Sarasota. Mobil Travel Guide has called Turtle
Beach the third nicest beach in the world (only the French Riviera and
one other exceed it). Drive for a half an hour and hike at the Myakka
River State Park. But watch for gators! Little dogs can be a yummy
snack! Great Jazz clubs, shopping, theater, and exciting city things can
be found in Sarasota proper.

Turtle Beach Resort
9049 Midnight Pass Rd.
Siesta Key, FL 34242
(941) 349-4554

Festivals/Happenings

Wine Festival (October); Summer Film Festival (August)
Santa Rosa Beach
Music, dancing, food and drink and wine tasting can be found at this festival in Town Center. Dogs are allowed on Walton County beaches with a leash, so you can walk your pet down to the shore after the festival or the film.

Film Festival
(904) 231-5424
Wine Festival
(904) 267-8092

Ft. Lauderdale Pet Show
Broward County Convention Center
Ft. Lauderdale, FL
(203) 563-2111

Cat Fanciers Association Annual Mtg.
Registry
Naples, FL
(908) 528-9797

Hotels/Motels
Howard Johnson Lodge   Amenities: H,S,NS   Cost: *
314 Miracle Strip Parkway
Ft. Walton Beach, FL 32548
(904) 243-6162

Quality Inn   Amenities: G.R.T   Cost: **
1208 N. Ocean Blvd.
Pompano Beach, FL 33952
(305) 782-5300

Econo Lodge   Amenities: G,R,T   Cost: *
28090 Quail's Nest Lane
Bonita Springs, FL 33923
(813) 947-3366

SOUTHEAST

Dog Friendly Beaches
St. Augustine/St. Augustine Beach
Ft. Lauderdale (restrictions apply)
Amelia Island/North Florida
Sanibel Island/Sanibel Island
Fernandina Beach/North Florida
Neptune Beach/Jacksonville
Atlantic Beach/Jacksonville
St. John's County Beach/South of Jacksonville
St. Augustine Beach/South of Jacksonville
Flagler Beach/ South of Jacksonville
Walton County Beaches/Northwest Florida
Cape San Blas Beach/Northwest Florida
Cedar Key Beach/Central Florida

Camping Information
Florida Campground Association
1638 N. Plaza Dr.
Tallahassee, FL 32308
(904) 656-8878

Georgia

Sights/Towns To See
Atlanta
Home of the 1996 Olympics, Atlanta is a town transformed. Stroll West Paces Ferry Road or Piedmont Avenue where you can find historic homes and antique shops galore. Just about any road off Peachtree Street will yield something interesting and a drive down this main street brings hundreds of restaurant and shopping choices. The Beverly Hills Inn welcomes your pet throughout your stay for a $10 fee. The Inn has period furniture, private balconies, and its own library!

Hotels/Motels

Beverly Hills Inn   Amenities: G   Cost: **
65 Sheridan Drive NE
Atlanta, GA 30305
(404) 233-8520

Quality Inn   Amenities: R,SA   Cost: **
330 Peachtree Street
Atlanta, GA 30308
(404) 577-1980

Savannah
One of the best preserved cities in the U.S., the architecture is a main reason to visit Savannah. It is home to the largest historic district in the nation. An interesting fact I stumbled upon is that Savannah claims to have the second largest **St. Patrick's Day** parade in the nation! They claim it is larger than Boston's parade, though this is unverified. Down by the riverfront there are always different festivals, including the **Irish Festival**, the **Jewish Food Festival**, etc. These festivals are all pet friendly and lots of fun. One of the best things to do with your pet is to take a walking tour of the historic part of the city.

Bed & Breakfast Inn   Amenities: G,R,T   Cost: **
117 W. Gordon St.
Savannah, GA 31401
(912) 238-0518

Quality Inn   Amenities: G,H,R,T   Cost: **
Route 5
Box 285
Savannah, GA 31408
(912) 964-1421

Arts & Crafts Festival (October)
St. Simons Island
In pet-friendly Neptune Park, this folk art, modern art, shopping, cultural exhibit, and food and drink filled festival is held every year. If you wait till the afternoon to go, you can walk your pet on Neptune Beach after 4:30 P.M.

Arts & Crafts Festival
(912) 638-9014

Dog Days (August)
Lumpkin
Westville Village, a reconstructed 1850 town, graciously opens its doors to pets on all occasions, especially this one. Interesting to visit anytime, it's especially nice when this arts, crafts, music and cutural festival is going on.

Westville Village
(912) 838-6310

Yellow Daisy Festival (September)
Stone Mountain
In a 50 mile radius of the Stone Mountain Park, the yellow daisy blooms every September. The Festival celebrates that blooming with local cuisine, horticultural competitions, arts and crafts, beer, food and wine. There are all sorts of activities at the Park, like golf and dining, but your pet can only be outside in certain places and The Stone

Mountain Inn on premises does not welcome pets. You can, however, seek lodging in Atlanta, only 16 miles away.

Yellow Daisy Festival
(770) 498-5690

Oktoberfest (October)
Savannah
They're having a lot of fun down here at the Rousakis Plaza on River Street in October. They've got the usual drinking, eating, German food, and music that you'd expect. They also have, the spokeswoman said with a laugh, the Wiener Dog Race. All dogs are, of course, welcome, but lots of dachshunds show up for this amusing competition. Held on the Savannah River, Oktoberfest is two fun-filled days of "Oompah" and beer.

Oktoberfest
(912) 234-0295

The Rose Festival (April)
Thomasville
A festival of beautiful blooms, as the name suggests. Pet-compatible, naturally!

Hotels/Motels
Susina Plantation Inn   Amenities: R,S,G   Cost: ***
Route 3, Box 1010
Thomasville, GA 31792
(912) 377-9644

Shoney's Inn   Amenities: R,G   Cost: *
305 Hwy 195
Thomasville, GA 31792
(912) 228-5555

State Botanical Gardens
2450 S. Milledge Ave.
Athens, GA
(404) 542-1244

Dog Friendly Beaches
Golden Isles/St. Simons
Jekyll Island Beaches
Cumberland Nat'l Seashore

Mississippi

Sights/Towns To See

Vicksburg
Site of one of the most important battles of the Civil War, history is preserved in the **Vicksburg National Military Park**, an informative site that is on the actual battlefield. Pets are welcome in this park which stretches for miles. Antebellum homes, casinos, and lots of good restaurants can be found in this historic city. There are several dog-friendly parks from which you might be able to catch the almost monthly fireworks that each casino provides as part of their respective anniversary celebrations.

The River Fest in March is one great big three-day outdoor party that welcomes pets. There are several flea markets nearby that welcome you and Fido as well.

Hotels/Motels
The Corners   Amenities: G,S,T   Cost:**
601 Klein Street
Vicksburg, MS 39180
(800) 444-7421
(601) 636-7421

Ramada Limited   Amenities: G,S,T,NS,OB   Cost:*
4216 Washington Street
Vicksburg, MS 39180
(601) 638-5750

Rowan Oak House
Oxford
Built in the 1840's, this small but historic house welcomes pets outside in the gardens and around the house, but not inside. The author William Faulkner lived and worked in this landmark home. There are a number of out buildings that you and the hound can visit too.

Rowan Oaks
(601) 234-3284

Elvis Presley Park and Birthplace
Tupelo
At last you can reminisce with Elvis! Not at Graceland, but here where it all began. This 15 acre site includes his birthplace house, a museum, giftshop and chapel. Pets are welcome.

Elvis Presley Birthplace
(601) 841-1245

Biloxi
The (regular) Walking and **Vieux Marche Walking Tours** show off the city at its finest. Pass the Art and Mardi Gras Museums, antique shops, the home of Mary Mahoney, and the Brielmaier, Scherer, and Clemens homes.

Visitor Center
(601) 374-3105
(601) 374-2717

Festivals/Happenings

Sand Sculpture Contest (September)
Biloxi
An unusually competitive event at which it was suggested to me that, while leashed dogs are allowed on Sand beach and at this event, we must take care to see that they don't change the outcome with any wet rearranging of sculptured sand just "for the halibut". I think you get my drift. It makes the participants crabby.

Sand Sculpture Contest
(800) 332-4653
(601) 896-2324

Steamboat and Floozy Race (June)
Natchez
Miss Under-the-Hill, the most representative of a typical olde-time floozy, is crowned at this event near Silver Street. The costumes are apparently something to see, as are the steamboats racing past this pet-friendly section of town. Lots of wonderful restaurants, gift and novelty shops can also be found here, by the Ole' Mississipi.

Biloxi Seafood Fest
Biloxi
Held in Point Cadet Plaza, there are all kinds of festivities throughout the day. Music, dancing, cultural events, arts and crafts and lots of seafood await the visitor.

Beach Convention and Visitor's Center
(800) 237-9493

Dog Friendly Beaches
Gulf beaches (All)
Nat'l Seashore Beaches (All)

SOUTHEAST

North Carolina

Sights/Towns To See

Asheville
Visit the magnificent Biltmore Estates. Although dogs are only allowed on the grounds, you might want to go in, in which case Don and Joan Tracy at the Dogwood promise to show your dog a good time while you're out exploring for a short while--could you ask for better Southern hospitality? Don't miss the Thomas Wolfe house, antique bookstore, or the world famous scenic Blue Ridge Parkway. Your dog will love the drive and the view of the highest peak east of the Mississippi, if you leave the AC on!

Hotels/Motels
The Dogwood Cottage Inn   Amenities: G,T,NS   Cost:**
40 Canterbury Rd.
Asheville, NC 28801
(704) 258-9725

Econo Lodge   Amenities: G,H,R,T   Cost:**
190 Tunnel Rd.
Asheville, NC 28805
(704) 254-9521

Spruce Pine/Little Switzerland
The yearly **Flume Fest** is a treat for all visitors to many sites around the area. There is a gem & mineral treasure hunt at the Emerald Village. The Emerald Village has a regular mine tour every day and you can buy buckets of dirt that has been excavated from the mine for five dollars. You then take a while and sort through this bucket looking for gems. Most people find interesting things; it's almost a guarantee I hear.

Flume Fest
(704) 765-6463

Hotels/Motels
Spruce Pine Motel   Amenities: G,T,NS   Cost:**
423 Oak Avenue
Spruce Pine, NC 28777
(704) 765-9344

Concord
All kinds of festivities occur in Frankliske Park, where you can always
bring your dog for a walk. The **Share Cabarrus Festival** brings food,
music, vendors, foot races, gold panning and much more to the park.
The **Western Fest** is held closer to fall as is the **Holiday Highlights**
where they elaborately adorn the regular walking path with Christmas
lights. It is so interesting that it takes more than an hour to see
everything on the short path.

Reed Gold Mine in nearby Stanfield is open for prospectors all week
long and they welcome your pet on a leash. Two dollars per pan
includes a complete 20-minute lesson in how to prospect.

Share Cabarrus Festival
Western Festival
Holiday Highlights
(704) 788-9840

Reed Gold Mine
9621 Reed Mine Rd.
Stanfield, NC 28163
(704) 786-8337

Hotels/Motels
Days Inn   Amenities: N/A   Cost:**
5125 Davidson Hwy.
I-85 & NC 73
Concord, NC 28027
(704) 786-9121

Festivals/Happenings

Annual Spring Kiln Opening
Creedmoor
Cedar Creek Gallery holds several events each year where they share the skill of the making of pottery with visitors as well as fun food, demonstrations, music, and more. Dogs are welcome to share the festivities, most of which occur outside. There is a large indoor gallery (dogs outside please) with the work of over 300 potters. Each fall there is a **National Teapot Show** as well, and you can always visit the **Museum of American Pottery** in an adjacent building. There is lots to see and do outdoors with your pet; and there are currently two Labs living at the gallery who know enough not to enter specific rooms.

Cedar Creek Gallery
(919) 528-1041

Hotels/Motels
Howard Johnson Lodge   Amenities: H,R,S,NS   Cost:**
1800 Hillandale Road
Durham, NC 27705
(919) 477-7381

The Anything That Floats Boat Parade
Asheville
Dogs are welcome at this crazy event in French Broad River Park. A boat parade and water show will entertain the two of you; and if you decide to enter you might win the $1000 Grand Prize!

Karen Cragnolin
(704) 252-8474

Music for A Sunday Evening In The Park
Greensboro
Several outdoor parks in the town of Greensboro sponsor these summer concerts for people and pooches (leashed, please).

Lynn Donovan
(910) 373-2549

Hotels/Motels
Econo Lodge   Amenities: H,R,S,NS   Cost:**
3303 Isler St.
Greensboro, NC 27407
(910) 852-4080

Charlotte Pet Expo
Charlotte
Games, contests, races and lots of fun are in store for your pet (and you!) in this two day fun fest in Charlotte.
Registration
(704) 543-3742

Hotels/Motels
Charlotte Hilton   Amenities: N/A   Cost:**
8629 J. M. Keynes Dr.
Charlotte, NC 28262
(704) 547-7444

Any & All Dog Show
Tryon Riding and Hunt Club
1 Depot St., P.O. Box 1095
Tryon, NC 28782
(800) 438-3681

Hotels/Motels
The Foxtrot Inn   Amenities: N/A   Cost:**
800 Lynn Road/ Rt. 108
P.O. Box 1561
Tryon, NC 28782
(704) 859-9706

Dog Friendly Beaches
Atlantic Beach
Cape Hatteras National Seashore (70 miles, all dog friendly!)
Cape Lookout Nat'l Seashore
Crystal Coast/Cartaret
Onslow County Beaches
Topsail Island Beaches

South Carolina

Sights/Towns To See

Charleston
This well preserved city beckons all who travel in the Southeastern US. Stroll the city and see hundreds of beautiful ante-bellum homes and public buildings. See the Isle of Palms, a secluded paradise with 7 miles of dog-friendly beach. Magnolia Plantations and Boone Hall (outside only) also allow leashed pets.

Charleston Landing zoo and park allow pets as well. Middleton Inn is an 18th century River Plantation with lovely river views, gardens, waterfront park areas, <u>and</u> **alligators**! It was suggested that dog owners be careful when walking by the river with Fifi; she could become a tasty snack for a hungry gator! By the same token, it is nice to leave the wild places and creatures to their own devices. I look forward to seeing happy alligators frolicing in their river home and not wrestling some moron in some hot, awful arena somewhere. Sorry, it was just waiting to be said...

Charleston Visitor's Center
(800) 868-8118

Hotels/Motels

The Indigo Inn	Amenities: N/A	Cost:**
1 Maiden Lane		
Charleston, SC 29401		
(803) 577-5900		

Middleton Inn	Amenities: N/A	Cost:**
Ashley River Rd.		
Charleston, SC 29407		
(803) 556-0500		

Hilton Head
One of the most popular resorts in the U.S., Hilton Head has golf, tennis, swimming, boating and dog friendly beaches in the off season. All the beaches (from Memorial Day thru Labor Day) allow leashed dogs before 10 AM and after 5 PM. From April 1st through Memorial day, dogs must be leashed but are allowed on beaches. On October 1st (thru March 31st) dogs can be off leash anywhere on any beach. One caveat: the Chamber of Commerce told me that there is a flea and sand fly problem at the beaches, so many hotels have decided not to allow pets as of June 1, 1996. Only Red Roof Inn still allows your pets.
Chamber of Commerce
(803) 785-3673

Hilton Head Island Realty
(800) 845-5552
These people will try and find a place for you, but you must pay $200 to have the room cleaned and exterminated after you leave.

Red Roof Inn   Amenities: N/A   Cost:**
5 Regency Pkwy
Hilton Head, SC 29928
(803) 686-6808

Festivals/Happenings
American Classic Tea Open House
A free tour of America's only tea plantation will reveal the history of tea and tea production. Tastings are available. Pets on leash welcome.

Charleston Tea Plantation
6617 Maybank Hwy.
Wadmalaw Island, SC 29487
(803) 559-0383

Fall Candlelight Tour of Homes & Gardens
Self-directed walking tour features a different street each night for a month. Historically and architecturally significant homes and beautiful gardens are featured as you stroll with your pet. Many homes might not allow Fido inside, but the walks are lovely...

The Preservation Society of Charleston
147 King Street
Charleston, SC 29401
(803) 722-4630

Springtime In The Falls
Giant yard sale and craft fair for the whole town. Live entertainment
and arts and crafts are the main attractions of this festival.

Calhoun Falls Town Hall
P.O. Box 452
Calhoun Falls, SC 29628
(864) 447-8512

Hotels/Motels
Econo Lodge   Amenities: G,R,T   Cost: *
719 Bypass 25 NE
Greenwood, SC 29646
(803) 229-5329

Dog Friendly Beaches
Charleston/ Isle of Palms
Hilton Head
Myrtle Beach
Pawleys Island/Georgetown area
Litchfield Beach/ Georgetown area
Debidue Beach/Georgetown area
Charleston Area Beaches

Tennessee

Sights/Towns To See

Dollywood

Dollywood, as you may know, is the creation of country singing star Dolly Parton. We all know her to be kind and generous and now that kindness extends to our furry friends. All are welcome at Dollywood, home of the Dollywood Express, an authentic steam train that allows dogs to ride. Country crafts, downhome cookin', music, magic, and fun await you and your pet.

1020 Dollywood Lane
Pidgeon Forge, TN 37863-4101
(800) DOLLYWOOD

Hotels/Motels
Holiday Inn Resort   Amenities: N/A   Cost:**
3230 Parkway
Pidgeon Forge,TN 37868
(800) HOLIDAY

Econo Lodge   Amenities: N/A   Cost:**
2440 Parkway
Pidgeon Forge, TN 36863
(615) 428-1231

Apple Valley Resort   Amenities: N/A   Cost:**
1850 Paul Drive
Jefferson City, TN 37760
(800) 545-8160

National Bird Dog Museum and Field Trial Hall of Fame
Grand Junction
Bird dog art, wildlife murals, and over 40 breeds of bird dog are
represented in this museum. The curator says that well behaved dogs
and their owners are welcome. Historical objects, game birds, wildlife
exhibits, and gift shop are found in this free exhibit.

National Bird Dog Museum and Field Trial Hall of Fame
State Hwy. 57
Grand Junction, TN 38008
(901) 764-2058, (901) 878-1168

Memphis Queen Line
Memphis
Elvis's home town, Memphis gets thousands of visitors each year.
Sorry, I checked. No Graceland. But don't despair, there's lots of
other fun things to do...Civil war sites...How about a Mississippi River
Cruise?! You have a choice of a 1 1/2 hour sightseeing cruise, a 2 hr.
sunset dinner cruise, or a Moonlight Music Cruise which is 2 hrs. on
Friday and 3 hrs. on Saturday. All welcome the dog, but he must be
picked up after and be leashed. Enjoy the floating gift shop and the
captain's booming voice as he tells of the river legends (the sightseeing
cruise only) and the cobblestones that are registered in National
Historic Places. See the oldest bridge on the Mississippi, Mud Island
(Sorry again, no pets on Mud Island), and the Pyramid.

Memphis Queen Line
(901) 527-5694

Brownestone Hotel   Amenities: S,R   Cost:**
300 N. Second
Memphis, TN 38105
(901) 525-2511
(800) 468-3515

Comfort Inn Airport Graceland   Amenities: S,T,R   Cost:**
2411 Winchester Rd.
Memphis, TN 38116
(901) 332-2370
(800) 365-2370

Festivals/Happenings

Ducks Unlimited (May)
Memphis
Sporting and wildlife festival. Vendors and demonstrations.
(901) 758-3711

Rock City's Enchanted Garden of Lights (November)
You and your best friend can stroll along the traditional trail now
decked out for the holidays. Although it is not much more than half a
mile, it is said that it takes most folks about an hour. Fairyland caverns
and Mother Goose Trail for the kiddies.

Rock City/Lookout Mountain
(706) 820-2531

International Country Music Fan Fair (Summer)
Nashville
Held on the Tri-State Fair grounds each year, it is a festival for the ears
for country music fans. Bring your pet. One of the few concerts in
Nashville the dog will be invited to.

International Country Music Fan Fair
Nashville, TN
(615) 889-7503

SOUTHEAST

MIDWEST

MIDWEST

Illinois
Indiana
Kentucky
Michigan
Ohio
Wisconsin

Hotel Cost Codes (for average one-night stay)

*	$30-60/night
**	$61-100/night
***	$101-150/night
****	$151 and up/night
W	Hotel has weekly rates only

Note: costs may vary by season.

Hotel Amenity Codes

A	Airport nearby
H	Handicapped access
HS	Hair salon on premises
G	Golf within 10 miles
NS	Non-smoking rooms available
OB	Facility is on the beach
P	Playground on premises
R	Restaurant on premises
S	Swimming on premises
SA	Sauna on premises
SK	Skiing within 25 miles
T	Tennis within 10 miles

MIDWEST

MIDWEST
Illinois

Sights/Towns To See

Galena
U.S. history and antiques are major attractions in Galena. Former resident Ulysses S. Grant left his mark on several buildings in town. (No, not "For a good time call...") His home, presidential campaign headquarters and other great edifices that Mark Twain, Abraham Lincoln, and Teddie Roosevelt (the only third party candidate ever to win the U.S. Presidency!) visited are there for all to enjoy. Hike Blanding's Landing, Apple River Canyon State Park, and downtown. You're right near Iowa in Galena, so check out what's to do in Iowa too.

Best Western Quiet House   Amenities:R   Cost:**
9915 Hwy 20 East
Galena, IL 61036
(815) 777-2577

Triangle Motel
(815) 777-2897

Festivals/Happenings

Berghoff Octoberfest
Chicago
German Food, arts and crafts, music, dancing, and of course beer and wine can be found at this Adams Street festival downtown in September. Pets are welcome.

Berghoff Oktoberfest
(312) 427-3170

Dog Day at Comiskey Park

Yea!!! Take me out to the ball game...Take me out to the park...Buy me some "Milkbones" (TM) and "Liv-A-Snaps" (TM)... I don't care if we never go back... They will have all kinds of dog snacks at this breakthrough day for the world of baseball and dogs. If you have a local ballpark nearby, ask them to sponsor a "Dog Day" too!

Comiskey Park
(312) 924-1000

Chicago - North Avenue Beach Festivals
Concerts in the Park (July/August)

Latin, classical, rock music for the eager listener can be found all summer long in North Avenue Beach. Since the beach is pet-friendly, so are the festivals. Concerts in the pet-friendly parks also take place at Promontory Park (July), South Shore Cultural (July), Lincoln Park Cultural, Margate Park, and Berger Park.

Mini-Festivals (August)

Children's activities, fun foods, street performances and smaller events fill the days of these mini-fests downtown.

Beach Poets (July)

Poets, drummers, and itinerant musicians ply their trade down at the North Avenue Beach day and night throughout this funky festival. Come on down with your new creation. Bring Fido; you know how he loves a good poetry reading.

WBBM Radio Beach Volleyball Tournaments (July)

Watch Chicago's best volleyball players compete in this grueling beach event for supreme net dominance over all who enter. Bring a cool drink for you and the pooch and enjoy! Please scoop!

Air and Water Show (August)

Sporting events, many of which can be observed from several onshore locations are the order of the day at this exciting event.

1600 N. Lakeshore Drive
North Avenue Beach
Downtown Chicago
(312) 747-2474

The Mayor's Office of Special Events
A Taste of Chicago (June)
Wonderful restauranteurs offer their most tasty creations at this downtown festival. It's all outside, so Fido is welcome.

Venetian Night (July)
Chicago is transformed into a small, old-world Italian town for this special event. Food, entertainment, and all the expected extras await the visitor.

Mayor's Cup Youth Soccer Festival (July)
An annual event, this competitive, but friendly event brings together soccer players of all generations to play and cheer for the players. Dogs on leash are welcome.

Chicago Jazz Festival (August)
Some of the biggest names in Jazz attend this large and varied festival in Grant Park. Dogs may be restricted from the area nearest the stage, but are allowed a bit further out in the pet-friendly park. That's good, because the noise right in front might hurt their ears or precipitate early deafness.

Contact the Mayor's Office of Special Events (MOSE) for details.
MOSE
(312) 744-3315
(312) 280-5740

Hotels/Motels
The Inn at University Village   Amenities:G,H,R   Cost:***
625 S. Ashland Ave.
Chicago, IL 60607
(312) 243-7200

The Essex Inn
800 S. Michigan Ave.
Chicago, IL 60605
(312) 939-2800

Amenities:N/A   Cost:***

The Ramada Inn Lakeshore
4900 S. Lakeshore Drive
Chicago, IL 60607
(312) 288-5800

Amenities:N/A   Cost:***

Ambassador West
1300 N. State Pkwy
Chicago, IL 60607
(312) 787-3700

Amenities:N/A   Cost:***

Pet Industry Christmas Trade Show (October)
Convention Center
Rosemont, IL
(312) 663-4040

Cat Fanciers Association Annual Meeting (June)
Chicago Marriot
Chicago, IL
(312) 528-9797

The Heart of Illinois Cluster/Dog Show
McLean County Fairgrounds

Chicagoland Family Pet Show (March)
Arlington Int'l Racecourse
Arlington Heights, IL
(708) 469-4611

Campgrounds
(All Accept Pets--only some are listed)
Arrowhead Acres/ Clinton
Bail's Timberline Lake/ St. Elmo
Wonderland/ Galena
Palace/ Galena

Benton KOA/ Benton
Camp Hauberg/ Port Byron
Camp Sycamore/ Sycamore
Crooked Tree/ Millbrook
Egyptian Hills Marina/ Creal Springs
Fox Valley/ Crystal Lake
Hayman's Shady Oak/ New Douglas
La Salle-Peru KOA/ North Utica
Waupecan Valley Park/ Morris

Pet-Friendly Chicago Parks
Many of these parks have water or beaches nearby. The hound is welcome in all the parks, but only on some of the beaches. Call the Park Service to double-check specific locations.

Park District/ Lakefront
(312) 747-2474

Grant Park
Berger Park
Clarendon Park
Lakeshore Park
Lincoln Park
Loyola Park
Margate Fieldhouse Park
Calumet Park
Daley Bicentennial Plaza
Jackson Park

Indiana

Sights/Towns To See

Bloomington
"Breaking Away", the wonderful film about growing up and coming of age in Indiana beneath the shadow of a grand university, was so heartwarming and interesting that it made me want to see the town of Bloomington. Visit the University grounds, have a stroll with Fido and explore what Indiana has to offer.

Hotels/Motels
Best Western   Amenities:G,R,SK   Cost:***
4501 E. Third St.
Bloomington, IN 47401
(812) 332-2141

Doggie Drive-Thru
South Bend
All-natural pet treats in this unnatural setting are only the beginning of the fun you and Fifi can have here! There is a dog/cat wash, a pet nanny for times when you need to shop, a swimming pool for the canines, and everything from wheat pizza to cheese fries for the discriminating dog or cat. Beef- or chicken-flavored ices for parties are just one of the amenities offered for entertaining from this house gone-to-the-dogs. It's worth a trip to South Bend just to visit this little bit of dog heaven!

Doggie Drive-Thru
50570 U.S. 31
South Bend, IN
(219) 271-0022

The Indiana Dunes National Lakeshore Park
Porter
Sand that sings to you as you walk, a place where your dog can swim (though not in high season), and moveable Mount Baldy, a "live" dune

that migrates several feet per year, are only some of the pleaasant surprises that await you in this National Park filled with fields, lakes and woodlands.

1100 North Mineral Springs Rd.
Porter, IN 46304
(219) 926-7561

Hotels/Motels
Econo Lodge   Amenities: H,R   Cost: **
3233 Lincoln Way W.
South Bend, IN 46628
(219) 232-9091

Festivals/Happenings

Balloon Festival (September)
Valparaiso
Daybreak launch of dozens of hot air balloons at the Porter County Fairgrounds. Fido might enjoy it if you brought breakfast and shared it with him (her).

Balloon Festival
(800) 283-8687

Canine Crusade (September)
Valparaiso
Annual pet walk to benefit the American Cancer Society. Sunset Hill Park is the perfect setting for friendly pet encounters.

Canine Crusade
(800) 283-8687

Harvest Festival & Antique Equipment Show (September)
Valparaiso
A celebration of rolling hills and rustic times, the Harvest Festival has demonstrations and displays of antique farm equipment and plenty of good fun. It is also held at Sunset Hill Park.

Harvest Festival
(800) 283-8687

Popcorn Festival (September)
Valparaiso
Porter County's most popular festival, it includes the Popcorn Panic (a 5K Run), the Popcorn Queen pageant, talent show, arts & crafts, kiddie run, tent dinners and much more! If you love popcorn, you'll love Valparaiso! Dogs are welcome.

Popcorn Festival
(800) 283-8687

Indiana State Fair (September)
Indianapolis
Auto thrill show, concerts, dance competition, carnival food and drink, horticultural exhibits and so much more can be found in this giant fair. There's something for everyone. Pets on leash welcome.

Indiana State Fair
(317) 927-1482

Wizard Of Oz Festival (September)
Chesterton
When I asked about whether pets were welcome at this festival, I half expected Elvira Gulch (having encountered her in other states and venues) to snap, "I'll get you, my pretty, and your little dog too!" No such luck. Seems I got Glinda, the Good Witch of the North, on the phone. She exclaimed, "How would we ever know if there were pets visiting, we have so many Totos competing for attention!" A good answer for the happiness of my dog, if ever I heard one. Dogs are very welcome at this event.

This is the largest Oz Fest in the world, with Munchkins and celebrities participating in autograph signings, the Fantasy Parade, the Town Crier competition and Look-Alike contests for all of the characters. "Toto, I...think we're in Kansas...uh...er...Indiana".

Wizard of Oz Festival
(800) 283-8687

Hotels/Motels
Ramada Inn   Amenities: G,R,S,NS   Cost: *
7813 Indianapolic Blvd.
Hammond, IN 46324
(219) 844-7780

Comfort Inn   Amenities: G,H,R,S,T   Cost: **
3880 W. 92nd St.
Indianapolis, IN 46268
(317) 872-3100

MIDWEST

Kentucky

Sights/Towns To See

Murray
Murray is the site of The National Boy Scout Museum, the second largest collection of Norman Rockwell paintings in the U.S., and is home to the Spinners, a group of storytellers that practice their art throughout town. If you like to antique, there are shops in nearby Hazel, Paris, and Mayfield as well as in town. Outdoor pet friendly activities include local baseball games and the Land between the Lakes (Kentucky and Barkley lakes). Land between the Lakes is a wildlife preserve that welcomes well-behaved pooches.

Hotels/Motels

The Diuguid House   Amenities: N/A   Cost:**
603 Main Street
Murray, KY 42071
(502) 753-5470

Murray Plaza Court   Amenities: N/A   Cost:**
P.O. Box 239
Murray, KY 42071
(502) 753-2682

Covington
Walking tours of incredible estates are a main activity here. Your pet is very welcome on any of these tours. At the Carneal Inn, the oldest and most revered historic landmark, Percy the dog is the canine concierge of the inn.

The Carneal Inn   Amenities: N/A   Cost:**
405 East Second St.
Covington, KY 41011
(606) 431-6130
(606) 581-6041

MIDWEST

Convention and Visitors Bureau
(606) 261-4677

Lexington
Bluegrass country. *De rigeur* for equestrians and a beautiful place for you and your best friend to visit. (Note: there are several horse shows listed in this guide because horse shows are almost always dog-friendly.) Visit the Kentucky Horse Center on the lovely drive known as the Paris Pike, the Kentucky Horse Park (camping available) or the Shaker village (Shakertown) south of Lexington.

Lexington Visitor's Bureau
(800) 848-1224

Hotels/Motels

Days Inn South   Amenities:R   Cost: ***
5575 Athens Boonesboro Rd.
Lexington, KY 40509
(606) 263-3100

Marriott's Griffin Gate   Amenities:R   Cost: ***
1800 Newtown Pike
Lexington, KY 40509
(606) 231-5100

Festivals/Happenings

Corn Island Storytelling Festival (September)
Louisville
First held in 1976, this is the largest story-telling festival in the world! The festival is sponsored by E.A.R.S., a group dedicated to the perpetuation of the art of story-telling. Fifty tellers from 5 continents create events in all the local and state parks. The best event is the Ghost Tale at Long Run State Park on Saturday night. Reminds me of camp days when we all tried to scare one another to death with our horror stories. You and your "Hound of the Baskervilles" can join the other lovers of magical tales and gather around the campfire to hear stories that will send shivers up your spine...

MIDWEST

Corn Island Storytelling Festival
(502) 245-0643

E.P. Tom Sawyer State Park
(502) 426-8950

Long Run Park
(502) 456-8100

International Banana Festival (September)
Fulton
Fulton, Kentucky is the Banana Capital of the World. Have I lost my mind? Gotten the facts mixed up? Nope, but there's a story involved. In the days when there was no formal refrigeration and people had to ship fruit and produce on blocks of ice, they often came directly up from Central America with bananas. By the time they reached Fulton, the much of the ice had melted and the crop was often lost. To combat this problem, Fulton created a major ice-making plant to re-ice the bananas for further shipment. More bananas were shipped to Fulton than anywhere in the world, and thus it acquired the title. Started in 1962, The Banana Festival is a lively event with music, fireworks, parades, and the best banana pudding anywhere. Many events occur in Pet-friendly Pontotoc Park where you and the pooch should have a great time!

International Banana Festival
(502) 472-2975

MIDWEST

Kentucky Bourbon Festival (September)
Bardstown
Headliners like Lorrie Morgan attract some 10,000 folks to this pet friendly event in the Bourbon Capital of the World. Exhibits, contests, great entertainment; and everything (except the distillery tours) is pet-friendly! Have a great time, but don't drink and drive (especially with Fido in the car).

Kentucky Bourbon Festival
(502) 349-0804

The Golden Armor Festival (September)
Radcliff
The longest running regional festival, The Golden Armor Festival is a salute to the men and women in the U.S. Armed Forces. The U.S. Army has a presence here at Fort Knox, and the community joins together in support of our brave young men and women. There is a community breakfast, floral show, golf tournament and a parade. Pets are welcome at just about everything.

The Golden Armor Festival
(800) 334-7540

Constitution Square Festival (September)
Danville
Historic re-enactments of life 200 years ago fulfill every anachronistic desire. Hammered dulcimer players, strolling minstrels, colonial games, storytelling, a fiddle contest, cultural and social demonstrations of life long ago delight you and your best friend. Held in Constitution Square downtown, a living village is set up complete with daily chores and community interrelationships.

Constitution Square Festival
(606) 239-7089

Kentucky State Fair (August)
Louisville
Twenty-eight competitive events from a horse show to a cooking show help entertain the 700,000 people who attend this event each year. Great food and music round out this elaborate event. Many people come for the World Championship American Saddlebred Horse Show or the mock trials. Pets welcome on leash.

Kentucky State Fair
(800) 626-5646

Hotels/Motels
Ramada Inn   Amenities: G,H,S,T,NS   Cost: *
523 North Third St.
Bardstown, KY 40004
(502) 349-0363

Ramada Hotel Airport East   Amenities: A,G,H,S,T,NS   Cost: *
1921 Bishop Lane
Louisville, KY 40218
(502) 456-4411

Michigan

Sights/Towns To See

Mackinaw Island
See the Grand Hotel, the Governor's summer home and Fort Mackinac on this island that almost seems to live in the 1880's -- when the Fort was built. No cars allowed on this island, only bikes or horseback can transport you faster than by foot. Many glacial rock formations can be seen here as well; Arch Rock and Skull Cave are two of the best known.

Hotels/Motels
Howard Johnson Lodge   Amenities: N/A   Cost:**
913 Boulevard Drive
St. Ignace, MI 49781
(906) 643-9700

Greenfield Village
Dearborn
Greenfield Village, an historical 1800's village, is almost a hundred acres of dog-friendly space. The original Wright Brothers' bicycle shop, the Henry Ford Museum, an operational steamboat and lots of historical buildings make this a good time for all.

Greenfield Village
P.O. Box 1970
Dearborn, MI 48121
(313) 271-1620

Dog Scout Camp
Swans Creek
Formed by Dog Scouts of America, this camp offers a chance for you and your dog to both learn and have fun. Water rescue, flyball, herding, and manners lessons are all on the schedule. There are also opportunities for dogs and their owners to learn sledding, but I think they'd have more fun with free-choice activities. I know *my dog* would

never willingly harness himself to a sled. There are also frisbee games and backpacking.

Dog Scout Camp
Camp Nahelu
Dog Scouts Of America
5307 W. Grand Blanc Rd.
Swans Creek, MI 48473

Festivals/Happenings

Straits Area Antique Auto Show & Swap Meet
St. Ignace
Over 3,000 antique and custom cars gather on this two mile stretch along with a swap meet, flea market, and toy and craft show. The Chamber of Commerce in St. Ignace says this is a great show, but to be careful that your pet is leashed and doesn't come into contact with any of these vintage autos (if you know what they mean). There is also a Labor Day Arts Dockside Show that your pet may attend as well.
Straits Show
(906) 643-8087
(906) 643-9402

St. Ignace Chamber of Commerce
(800) 338-6660

Maze of The Planets
East Tawas
Dogs are welcome at this unusual place, if you clean up after them. The walls are over 7 feet tall in this wooden maze that leads you through with astronomy questions! Even some NBA players couldn't see over them! You take a quiz card in with you and answer the questions as you search for the nine planets and a way out!

Maze of The Planets
(517) 362-2111

MIDWEST

The Mystery Spot
St. Ignace
Optical and physical sensations meant to challenge your senses and make you wonder are found here along with mini-golf, souvenirs, gift shop and picnic facilities. Dogs are welcome on some of the tours of this mystery spot.

Mystery Spot
US 2 West
St. Ignace, MI
(906) 643-8322

Mushroom Festival (May)
Mesick
A parade, craft show, flea market, dances, softball games, beer tent and "Mud-buster" Races all welcome you and your dog. There is a Largest Mushroom contest as well. These mushrooms are not the typical _Agricaris campestris_ that we see in large numbers at the supermarket. No, these are tasty and precious Morels!

Mushroom Festival
(616) 885-1280

Tulip Time Festival (May)
Holland
Why fly to Europe when we have a great tulip festival right here in our own Holland! A week of shows and displays, the Pretplaats (place to have fun) and the Kinderplaats (place for kids) keep everybody busy and amused within the five mile radius that this big festival encompasses! Of course the pet is welcome!

Tulip Time
(800) 822-2770

Hotels/Motels
Holland Fairfield Inn   Amenities: S,NS,H   Cost:**
2854 W. Shore Drive
Holland, MI 49424
(800) 228-2800

MIDWEST

Knights Court   Amemities: S,NS,H   Cost:**
422 E. 32nd St.
Holland, MI 49423
(800) 843-5644

The UKC All-Breed Dog Show (May)
Berrien Springs
Detroit Kennel Club Dog Show (March)
The UKC All Breed Dog Show (January)
Detroit
These three Dog Shows are unusually pet-friendly. It's a nice to see that some dog shows will allow pets and adopted dogs to attend and socialize. Contact the very pleasant UKC at the number below for more information.

The United Kennel Club (UKC)
(616) 343-9020

Hotels/Motels
The Westin Hotel   Amenities: R,S,NS,H   Cost:****
Renaissance Center
Detroit, MI 48243
(313) 568-8000

The Suburban House   Amenities: S   Cost: **
16920 Telegraph
Detroit, MI 48219
(313) 535-9646

Dulcimer Festival (May)
Caseville
Gathering groups of dulcimer players in Sleeper State Park sweeten the air with Renaissance sounds. Rover will love it! There is also an arts and crafts show and sale that accompanies this musical event. There is even camping in the park and a special concert given at night for the campers.

Sleeper State Park
(517) 856-4411

Pasty Bake (May)
St. Ignace
The dog will love you for this one!!! See the Paul Bunyan shop employees and helpers create the largest "Pasty" ("a" as in Akron) in the world. They set the Guinness Book Of World Records on its ear every year with this largest of MEAT PIES!!! Fido is drooling already because he knows that everybody gets to eat some after it has been measured and is official. There are eating contests and other activities as well. Make sure you keep the hound on leash and away from the food; bring him his portion away from other eaters who might be disturbed. We want to be invited back, don't we?

Pasty Bake
(800) 338-6660

Abbott's Magic Get-Together (July)
Colon
This annual gathering of thousands of magicians from around the world has been going on for over 60 years! Many shows are at the local high school and welcome quiet, leashed, well-behaved pets. (Please abide by the request that pets be quiet; magicians can not afford to lose their concentration during a performance.) Learn sleight-of-hand at workshops, purchase your own bag of tricks at the fair and sale that accompany this unusual event, or just marvel at the prestidigitation. Lots of fun all over town!

Abbott's Magic Get-Together
(616) 432-3235

Ice Sculpture Spectacular (January)
Plymouth
Watch the creation of amazing creatures by world-class sculptors. Incredible ideas take form at this town-wide outdoor spectacular. Chisels and chain saws help form 200+ sculptures in Kellogg Park and along the sidewalks downtown. Baking and gingerbread house contests round out the entertainment.

Chamber of Commerce
(313) 453-1540

MIDWEST

Cereal Festival (June)
Battle Creek
The World's Longest Breakfast Table (three blocks long) is created in downtown Battle Creek by the Big Three cereal makers in town; Kelloggs, Post and Ralston. The second Saturday in June is the time each year that you can have your FREE breakfast downtown! The dog may come on leash as long as there are no problems. My Ted would enjoy this; he likes his Cheerios or Special K each morning (skim milk and no sugar, of course). "The Best To You *This* Morning" from the best cereal makers in town!

Cereal Festival
(616) 962-8400

Turtlellen, A Canine Bakery
Whitehall
Party on, pups! Just order your cake early so that it will arrive fresh from this canine bakery. Made with love for only $35 (plus $4.00 shipping). What more could you ask for?!

Turtlellen
P.O. Box 353
Whitehall, MI 49461
(616) 893-3800

<u>Great Walking/Driving Tours</u>

Midland
Pick up a map at the Midland Center for the Arts and hop in the car for a look at almost 60 beautiful homes and buildings, all designed by one good architect, Alden Dow (son of the founder of Dow Chemical Company). This driving tour can be taken at any time of year, but the annual tour time is in the fall.

Convention & Visitor's Center
(800) 678-1961

MIDWEST

Marshall

An annual tour in the fall has thousands of visitors, but again, you can do this anytime. Walk or drive this tour of 135 historic structures.

Chamber of Commerce
(800) 877-5163

MIDWEST

Ohio

Sights/Towns To See

Pet FriendlyWineries
Wineries provide an excellent venue for relaxing with your pet. Many of these friendly places allow you to taste different wines, attend special festivals, pick your own fruit (depends on the type of fruit), picnic with the hound and peruse gift possibilities in their shops. Fido is seldom allowed on the tour of the inside of the winery because of health regulations, but he won't mind because there's lots of other things to do. All these wineries were very pet-friendly and Kelley's Island Winery was particularly nice when we contacted them.

Greco Winery
French grapes
Middletown
(513) 539-8768

Limpert Winery
Native American grapes
Westlake
(216) 871-0035

John Christ Winery
French, Native American grapes
Avon Lake
(216) 933-9672

Kelley's Island Winery
French, European grapes
Kelley's Island
(419) 746-2537

Klingshirn Winery
Native American, French grapes
Avon Lake
(216) 933-6666

Wyandotte Winery
French, Native American grapes
Gahanna
(614) 476-3624

Festivals/Happenings

Zuccini Festival
Eldorado
Ever had a zuccini milkshake? Well get ready to try one at this festival...It's a must! They are made with zuccini, milk and special spices. The milkshake actually has more of a cinnamon taste than zuccini, and a good one. Every other type of baked, fried, or constructed good that can be zuccinied, is.
(513) 273-3281

Canal Festival (August)
Coshocton
A Saturday morning parade starts off the festivities that celebrate the 1830's canal boat era with boat rides, crafts and entertainment in Historic Roscoe Village.
(800) 877-1830

Meteor Shower Campout (August)
Waynesville
Timed perfectly with the beginning of the Perseid meteor shower (Aug. 11-15) that occurs every year right before my birthday, this Caesar Creek State Park campout includes constellation as well as nocturnal animal info and you and your pet are welcome to come and gaze. Lots of fun!
(513) 897-2437

Pumpkin Show (October)
Circleville
Ohio's oldest and largest harvest event celebrates almost 100 years of fall fun. Seven parades, pumpkins in greater numbers than can be imagined, squash, gourds, food, and arts and crafts create a marvelous fall event.
(614) 474-7000

Dayton Kennel Club Show (June)
Dayton, OH

Cluster In The Hills Dog Show (May)
Brush Run Park
St. Clairsville, OH

Contact:
Fort Steuben KA
St. Clairsville KC

The Greater Cincinnati Memorial Day Cluster Dog Show(May)
Butler County Fairgrounds
Rte. 4
Hamilton, OH

Contact:
Norma Woolf
(513) 474-3378
Steve Davidson
(513) 724-1516

Company Tours
Ohio is home to much industry, and many of the manufacturers would like to share some of their secrets with you. I have toured several of these companies in different states. The breweries and the instrument makers are most interesting. Most of these tours are not friendly to pets as large as my Ted, but some may allow little dogs. Anyway, I thought they looked like fun so I included them.

United Musical Instruments (Brass instruments)
Cleveland
(216) 946-6100

Quaker Square (Quaker Oats)
Akron
(330) 253-5970

Anheuser-Busch (Brewery)
Columbus
(614) 888-6644

General Motors (Car maker)
Warren
(216) 824-5000

The Plain Dealer (Newspaper)
Cleveland
(216) 344-4230

Covered Bridges
Humpback Bridge/Vinton County
Germantown Bridge/Montgomery County
Island Run Bridge/Morgan County
Scofield Bridge/Brown County

Campgrounds (Pet-friendly)
There are about 140 campgrounds in Ohio, more than half of which are
pet friendly. Selected ones are listed.

Airport RV Park/Hebron
Audubon Lakes Campground/Geneva
Bass Lake Family Recreation/Springfield
Bay Shore/Andover
Camp America/Oxford
Camp Toodik/Loudonville
Charlie's Place/Lisbon
Dayton Tall Timbers KOA/Dayton
E-Z Camp Area/Wapakoneta

MIDWEST

Foxfire Family Campground/Nevada
Honey-Do Campground/Spencer
Lazy R/Granville
Top 'O The Caves/Logan
Yogi Bear's Jellystone Park/Cinncinnati

Wisconsin

Sights/Towns To See

The Velodrome
Kenosha
Classic bicycle races can be seen every Tuesday in the summer in this oldest of all velodromes in the U.S. Come on down and bring your leashed friend. Free Admission.
The Velodrome
(414) 652-2522

Riveredge Galleries and Sculpture Garden
North of Kenosha, in Manitoc County lies a wonderful pet-friendly gallery run by Christopher Baugniet. A number of festivities here in the summer are held outside in the sculpture gardens. Larger dogs are welcome at these events. But small dogs (e.g. carryable) may peruse the galleries' contents at will!
Riveredge Galleries
432 E. Main St.
P.O. Box 297
Mishicot, WI 54228
(414) 755-4777

Dog Days of Wisconsin (August)
Dousman
A three day camp where you can hike, boat or swim with your canine companion. Relax and play or make a clay paw print for your dog to keep. There are a myriad of activities in arts and crafts area. Near Waupaca, WI.
Camp Helen Brachman
West 359 S 4125 Bowe Ct.
Dousman, WI 53118
(800) CAMP-4-DOGS
(414) 444-0437

White Cap Mountain
Montreal
Dogs are welcome to enjoy downhill skiing with their owners at this largest ski resort in Wisconsin! It's better not to attempt to outfit them with their own boots and skis. Just be happy that they can accompany you while you ski.

Whitecap Mt.
(800) 933-SNOW
(715) 561-2776

Hotels/Motels
Mt. Retreat Chalet   Amenities: N/A   Cost: ***
Montreal, WI
(715) 561-2776

Festivals/Happenings

Clown Town Colossal (Summer)
Delevan
This is the home of the Clown Hall of Fame and the festivities continue throughout the year, but clown performances can be seen mostly in the summer. This Colossal is held outside every year and dogs are invited (outside only please). Expect the usual shenanigans as well as an afternoon pie fight and continual clown shows.

The Clown Hall of Fame
(414) 728-9075

Concerts on the Square (Summer)
Madison
The Wisconsin Symphony Orchestra delights listeners with the strains of classical music on the State Capitol grounds several times over the summer. Vendors sell boxed dinners or you can bring your own for a romantic time with Fido and friends. There is a preference that dogs stay with their owners in the closed street section instead of the lawn, but there is no hard and fast rule as of this writing.

MIDWEST

Hotels/Motels
Econo Lodge　　　　Amenities: G,H,R,SK　　Cost:**
4726 E. Washington Ave.
Madison, WI 53704
(701) 572-4242

Ramada Limited　　Amenities: A,G,S,T,NS,SK　Cost:**
3841 E. Washington Ave.
Madison, WI 53704
(608) 244-2481

Pops Band Performances (Summer)
Kenosha
These concerts are held in the cool of the summer evening in
Sesquicentennial Band Shell in downtown Kenosha.　Dogs are
welcome.　What a nice way to end a summer day!

Pops Performances
(414) 657-5031

Food, Folks, and Spokes (July)
Kenosha
The Fresca Pro-Am Bicycle Race is the main event in July in this very
bicycle oriented town.　Lots of food stands supply a "Taste of
Kenosha" to this entertainment extravaganza.　The Sports and Health
Fair continues while the streets are shut down for the big race.　All you
science types can come on down on your Carnot cycle and find a
common hollow log for you and Fido to sit on.

Fresca Pro-Am
(414) 657-5031

Hotels/Motels
Budgetel Inn　　　Amenities: N/A　　　　Cost:**
7540 118th Ave.
Kenosha, WI 53142
(414) 857-7911

Holiday Inn   Amenities: N/A   Cost:**
5125 6th Ave.
Kenosha, WI 53140
(414) 658-3281

Milwaukee Family Pet Show (October)
Held at the Wisconsin State Fair Park near the end of October, there are
numerous contests and fun things to entertain both you and your pet.

Wisconsin State Fair Park
(800) 946-4611

Assn. of Wisconsin Tourist Attractons
(608) 253-5100

Hiking Information
Ice Age Park & Trail Foundation
(414) 691-2776

State Parks & Forests
(608) 266-2181

Wisconsin Duck Boat Tours
Wisconsin Dells
(608) 254-8751

Dog Friendly Beaches
Lake Mendota/Madison
Maslowski Beach/Ashland
Bayview Park/Ashland
Lake Delton/Wisconsin Dells

Camping Information
(608) 266-2181

SOUTH-CENTRAL

SOUTH-CENTRAL

Arkansas
Kansas
Louisiana
Missouri
Oklahoma
Texas

Hotel Cost Codes (for average one-night stay)

*	$30-60/night
**	$61-100/night
***	$101-150/night
****	$151 and up/night
W	Hotel has weekly rates only

Note: costs may vary by season.

Hotel Amenity Codes

A	Airport nearby
H	Handicapped access
HS	Hair salon on premises
G	Golf within 10 miles
NS	Non-smoking rooms available
OB	Facility is on the beach
P	Playground on premises
R	Restaurant on premises
S	Swimming on premises
SA	Sauna on premises
SK	Skiing within 25 miles
T	Tennis within 10 miles

SOUTH-CENTRAL

SOUTH CENTRAL
Arkansas

Sights/Towns To See
Helena
There is a lovely trail on the Mississippi River that has an elevated boardwalk where runners can be found in the early hours. Many antebellum homes, historic places to visit, a Confederate cemetery and casinos galore await the traveler. In October there is a world class **Blues Festival** that draws folks from everywhere. The Festival takes place on Cherry Street and your pet is welcome! You can stroll by or stay and enjoy the wonderful sounds. So many people want to attend this festival that one of the pet friendly inns in town, The Edwardian Inn, has to have a lottery for rooms that weekend. The Edwardian Inn is a stunning, stately home with large guest rooms, a large rotunda, and two verandas wrapping around both sides of the house. Victorian era furnishings and a very pleasant proprietor make this a great place to stay. Send in your card in time for the drawing!

The Edwardian Inn
317 South Biscoe
Helena, AR 72342
(501) 338-9155

Festivals/Happenings

Annual Old Timer's Day Arts & Crafts Festival
Van Buren
300+ Arts & Crafts exhibitors from a seven-state area, good food, entertainment, and children's carnival are found at this yearly event. There is a larger version of this festival, held in October of each year, as well.

Old Timer's Day
(501) 474-0510

SOUTH-CENTRAL

Annual Free State of Yell Fest
Dardanelle
5K Run, volleyball, horshoes, tug-of-war, live entertainment, ugly dog contest (only enter your dog if he/she is very secure--could stunt his/her emotional growth...), fireworks, and a Yelling Contest the likes of which you may never see again.

Chamber of Commerce
P.O. Box 208
Dardanelle, AR 72834
(501) 229-3328

Bluegrass & Country Music Festival
Judsonia
Friendly Acres City Park holds this annual festival of old and new bluegrass and country. Lots of good eats and live entertainment as you sit on a blanket with your pooch.

Bluegrass Festival
(501) 729-5191

Picklefest
Atkins
State Pickle capital celebrates with tours of Atkins Pickle Company (no dogs for the tours) and pickle-eating contests, pickle-juice drinking contests, arts & crafts, softball tournament, and children's games. Little Mr. and Miss Pickle are crowned at this event.

Atkins Picklefest
(501) 641-2576

Hotels/Motels
Ramada Inn   Amenities: S,A,H,T,R,P,NS Cost: *
I-40 and U.S. 64
Conway, AR 72032
(501) 329-8392

SOUTH-CENTRAL

Ramada Inn Airport   Amenities: S,A,H,G,R,NS   Cost: *
5103 Towson Ave.
Fort Smith, AR 72901
(501) 646-2931

Comfort Inn   Amenities: H,R   Cost: *
107 S. Rand Drive
Searcy, AR 72143
(501) 279-9100

Dog Friendly Beaches
Table Rock Lake

cathy®   **by Cathy Guisewite**

CATHY © Cathy Guisewite. Reprinted with
permission of UNIVERSAL PRESS SYNDICATE.
All rights reserved.

Kansas

Sights/Towns To See

Abilene

Home to great mansions, museums, galleries, and interesting getaways like the Excursion train, Abilene is pet-friendly. You and the pooch can stroll the Heritage Center complex which includes the County Historical Museum and the Museum of Independent Telephony (antique telephone exhibit). Also found at the center are the Burkland Historical Store (transported to be at this site with other articles of history), the Pritchard Barn, and the C.W. Parker "Carry-Us-All" (the early "carousel"). You might want to have someone wait with the hound if you decide to check out any of the buildings that don't permit pets.

Abilene is also the home of Dwight D. Eisenhower, one of our most beloved Presidents. The grounds of the Eisenhower Center allow pets, but the home is off limits. Olde Town Abilene is an outdoor recreation of the town in the 1860's. Stroll past the restored historical homes and buildings with Fido. It's a nice place.

Abilene Visitor's Center
(800) 569-5915

WaKeeney

WaKeeney boasts bigger farms than some of our U.S. states. "The Christmas City of The High Plains", WaKeeney had a downtown holiday display designed, in 1950, for their 40 ft. tree. And every season, fresh garlands and wreaths, bows and lights adorn 3 miles of downtown; 2000 regular 40 watt colored light bulbs on the tree alone! They claim to be the brightest lights between Kansas City and Denver! Wonder if you can see them from space?

The dog is welcome at the Cottonwood Hollow Stable where they display and raise exotic animals, as well as at Castle Rock (a natural formation in a small park), and at the KOA campground nearby.

SOUTH CENTRAL

Wakeeney Economic Development
(913) 743-5785

Festivals/Happenings

Renaissance Festival (September)
Bonner Springs
A 16th century village celebrating the harvest awaits your visit. This is one of the only Renaissance festivals that allows pet, so go and make the most of it! Great food, crafts and entertainment.

Renaissance Festival
(800) 373-0357

Ohio Days (July)
Waverly
Over 100 years of this annual celebration have brought excitement to all (and their pets) who've attended. Parade, pancake *feed* (a vivid image to remind me to use control), baby show, ice cream social, live band, dancing and fireworks are promised over the two July days.

Ohio Days
(316) 364-2002

Riverfest (September)
Leavenworth
Outhouse Races (Hmm...), aircraft display, arts and crafts, rides and children's carnival are just some of the interesting activities this combination of three festivals has to offer. My favorite, from the Buffalo Bill Days (now part of Riverfest), is still the 450-foot long banana split! I can see my Ted just standing underneath waiting for drips...

Visitor's Center
(800) 844-4114

SOUTH-CENTRAL

Poinsettia Festival (November)
Lawrence
Downtown holiday festival featuring thousands of red poinsettia, in shops, restaurants, museums, and the Kansas Turnpike toll booths. An old fashioned Christmas parade, concert, vespers, living Nativity, and stage and outdoor shows are all part of this event.

Poinsettia Festival
(913) 865-4497

Pioneer Harvest Fiesta (October)
Fort Scott
Threshing, grinding of grain, lumber sawing and other 19th century chores send the observer back in time. Antique and classic tractor pulls, horse-drawn equipment and railroad cars highlight this "Fiesta" at the Bourbon County Fairgrounds.
Pioneer Harvest Fiesta
(800) 245-3678

Art Show at the Dog Show
11301 West 37th St. N.
Wichita, KS 67205
(316) 722-6181

Hotels/Motels
Ramada Inn   Amenities: H,R,S,NS   Cost: *
101 S. 3rd St.
Leavenworth, KS 66048
(913) 651-5500

Econo Lodge   Amenities: G,H,R,S,T   Cost: *
1240 SW Wanamaker Rd.
Topeka, KS 66604
(913) 273-6969

Comfort Inn   Amenities: G,H,R   Cost: *
4849 S. Laura
Wichita, KS 67216
(316) 522-1800

SOUTH-CENTRAL

Louisiana

Sights/Towns To See

THE PLANTATIONS
Ormond Plantation/Destrehan Plantation
Both can be seen from River Road and are beautiful. Ormond might be coaxed into taking you and your pet overnight at their B & B, and you both may walk the grounds. Destrehan, the site of "Interview With The Vampire", will not allow you to walk the grounds with a pet, but you can admire it from the front. Probably better that way; I don't want anyone to *really* relive this particular film, just see the plantation where it was filmed.

Destrehan Plantation
13034 River Rd.
Destrehan, LA
(504) 764-9315

Ormond Plantation
13786 River Rd.
Destrehan, LA
(504) 764-8544

Tezcuco Plantation
Greek Revival style home built in 1855, Tezcuco is adorned with wrought iron trimmed galleries, and ornate friezes and medallions. There are tours, a restaurant, and a gift shop. Best of all, you and the hound are welcome at this plantation which is also a B&B!! Use this as a base and take scenic drives through and by all of the plantations in the area! (Approx. 1 hr. from New Orleans)

Texcuco Plantation   Amenities:R   Cost: ***
3138 Hwy. 44
Darrow, LA 70725
(504) 562-3929

Oak Alley Plantation
A well recognized plantation, Oak Alley has the most stunning approach you have ever seen. It has 28 great oak trees with spanish moss curving over the drive to the mansion. It is a shot that you have seen many times in movies and on television. You are allowed to stop and photograph it from the driveway with your pet. Pets may not go in however.

Oak Alley
3645 Hwy 18
Vacherie, LA
(800) 442-5539

Houmas House Plantation and Gardens
Built in 1840, Houmas House has an exquisite white double wrap-around porch displaying (what I call) antebellum Georgian architecture. The state's largest sugar plantation in the 1800's, it is rich in serenity, beauty, and authentically dressed southern belles guide you through the house. Your dog is welcome on the grounds, but not in the house.

Houmas House
40136 Hwy 942
Burnside, LA
(504) 522-2262

Festivals/Happenings

New Orleans
Krewe of Barkus (April/March)
People getting themselves in the mood for Mardi Gras do some strange things. The Krewe of Barkus is no exception. Dogs are the feature of this parade, but not au naturel. No, they must be swathed in (annoyed by) the obligatory sartorial and tonsorial splendor (bizarre mess) that characterizes the fun-filled (booze-laden) days that precede the king of all debauchery festivals, Mardi Gras. On a toot already? Always imagined Fifi as Queen Elizabeth? This is the place, now is the time. You'll see dogs in every costume and hairdo imagineable. Walk your pooch in Coliseum park afterward so he doesn't ruin Grandma's old

petticoat on the way home. Actually it's all good fun (for some people). Just kidding. Really.

French Quarter Festival (April)
Phydeaux is invited to this outdoor extravaganza that features incredible cajun and creole cooking on the streets as well as jazz (as only New Orleans can offer) on just about every corner. Walk down Bourbon Street and drink in the sights and sounds as you eat blackened something-or-other with your dog. He won't know the difference.

French Quarter Festival
100 Conti Street
New Orleans, LA 70130
(504) 522-5730

Church Point Buggy Festival (May)
Church Point
Exquisite 18th and 19th century horse-drawn carriages are reminders of the pleasant aspects of the Old South. Church Point was the last town in Louisiana to stop using buggies in favor of the horseless carriage after the turn of the century. There are French, Cajun and several other ethnic festivals within this one. A Queen's pagent, parade, hourly live entertainment, a French accordian contest, and arts & crafts highlight this festival.

Hotels/Motels
Prytania Inn   Amenities:G,R,T   Cost:**
1415 Prytania St.
New Orleans, LA 70130
(504) 566-1515

B&B at The Chimes   Amenities:G,R,T   Cost:**
1360 Moss St.
P.O. Box 52257
New Orleans, LA 70152-2257
(504) 488-4640

SOUTH-CENTRAL

Quality Inn   Amenities:G,R,T   Cost:**
3900 Tulane Ave.
New Orleans, LA 70119
(504) 486-5541

Glimmer Inn   Amenities:G,R,T   Cost:**
1631 Seventh Street
New Orleans, LA 70115
(504) 897-1895

Dog Friendly Beaches
Grand Isle Beach/East
Holly Beach/West

Missouri

Sights/Towns To See

Silver Dollar City
Branson
A great adventure with a Dixie Stampede, the Grand Palace, and other events. Pets on leash are allowed in most outdoor areas.
HCR 1
P.O. Box 791
West Hwy 76
Branson, MO 65616
(800) 952-6626

The Dog Museum
St. Louis
Dedicated entirely to dogs, this museum has ever changing displays on different themes, most recently "Dogs of War". The thing to do on a summer trip-tickets can be hard to come by.
1721 S. Mason Rd.
St. Louis, MO 63131
(314) 821-3647

Hotels/Motels
Comfort Inn   Amenities: G,H,R   Cost: **
12031 Lackland Rd.
St. Louis, MO 63146
(314) 878-1400

Howard Johnson Hotel   Amenities: H,R,NS   Cost: **
5915 Wilson Ave.
St. Louis, MO 63110
(314) 645-0700

The Three Dog Bakery
St. Louis
A wonderful idea come to fruition -- A Bakery for Dogs! Lots of luscious treats baked especially for dogs, but that humans can eat as well. Dogs may come in and choose their own tempting treats for themselves. With names like Snicker Poodles, Rollovers, Big Scary Kitty cookies, and made-from-scratch biscuits can you not be excited?!! Sarah, Dottie and Gracie, the spokesdogs for Three Dog Bakery wouldn't have embarked on such a venture if it weren't woof it!

If you can't visit this adorable bakery, send for their biscuit-of-the-month club which offers a 3-lb. bag of different flavor, all-natural biscuits every month for a year!

Three Dog Bakery
4116 Pennsylvania Ave.
Kansas City, MO
(800) 487-3287

Hotels/Motels

Ramada Inn Southeast 1	Amenities: N/A	Cost:***
6101 E. 87th St.		
Kansas City, MO 64138		
(816) 765-4331		

Econo Lodge	Amenities: N/A	Cost:**
8500 E. 350 Hwy		
Kansas City, MO 64133		
(816) 353-3000		

Festivals/Happenings

Branson Music Fest (June)
Branson is the place to be in Missouri. Musical headliners from around the world perform here on a regular basis. While dogs are not allowed in the performance halls, all outdoor affairs are fair game. This particular festival is geared for those travelling by RV. Branson Music Fest allows dogs at the concerts and they are bussed with their owners

from the RV site to the different sites in the area where food, music, and festivities are held.

Jayco Jafari Club
P.O. Box 192
Osceola, IN 46561
(219) 258-0591

Hotels/Motels
Econo Lodge   Amenities: N/A   Cost:**
230 S. Wildwood Dr.
Branson, MO 65616
(417) 336-4849

Ramada Limited   Amenities: N/A   Cost:**
245 North Wildwood Dr.
Branson, MO 65616
(417) 336-6646

Port of Lights (November/December)
Kimberling City
Annual holiday drive-through display of lights and animated figures the likes of which you may not see again. Try and estimate the number of bulbs and determine the amount of wattage being used. No, that's boring. The dog does that all the time when you're out driving in the car. (OK, prove he doesn't...) Just enjoy.

Chamber of Commerce
(417) 739-2564

Dog Friendly Malls
Tangier Outlet Mall/Branson
Grand Village Mall/Branson
Factory Merchants Mall/Branson

Dog Friendly Parks
Busiek State Forest
Mark Twain National Forest
Paul Henning National Forest
Table Rock Lake State Park

Dog Friendly Beaches
Warsaw/Truman Lake
Stockton/Stockton Lake
Kimberling City/Table Rock Lake
Karsen/Lake of the Ozarks

Oklahoma

Sights/Towns To See

Wichita Mountains Wildlife Refuge
Lawton
Hikes and interpretive tours show you unique rock formations, lakes, buffalo, longhorn sheep, elk and other wildlife on this 60,000 acre preserve. There is a great 10 minute scenic drive up Mt. Scott that affords a different vantage point to the traveler.

Hotels/Motels
Holiday Inn   Amenities: N/A   Cost:**
3134 Cache Rd.
Lawton, OK 73505
(405) 353-1682

Festivals/Happenings

Ardmore Birthday Party (May)
Ardmore
Arts & crafts fair, concert in the park, hot air balloons, an evening Street Dance, Breakfast in Central Park, walking and driving tours of historic downtown buildings and homes from the late 1800's, and the final cake-cutting ceremony are events to which Fido is invited.
(405) 223-7765

Hotels/Motels
Holiday Inn   Amenities: N/A   Cost:**
2705 Holiday Dr.
Ardmore, OK 73401
(405) 223-7130

Sanders Family Bluegrass Festival (May)
Mcalester
Bring a blanket and relax with your pal to the strains of happy music. Family show featuring bluegrass musicians, concessions and RV hookups. 5 miles west on US-270.
(918) 423-4891

Hotels/Motels
Days Inn   Amenities: N/A   Cost:**
Rt. 8 / Box 155
Mcalester, OK 74501
(918) 426-5050

Fun Fest (June)
Pryor
This particular fest contains fertilizer put to good use as chips in the cow patty bingo game that runs throughout the day. As a kid, I always liked the bingo pieces cause you could see through 'em. Guess that doesn't work here. The entertainment includes children's games, live music, Amish bake sale, and arts and crafts. I must say, the Oklahomans know how to have fun. There is more to do here than just about anywhere.

Hotels/Motels
Pryor House Motor Inn   Amenities: N/A   Cost:**
123 S. Mill St.
Pryor, OK 74361
(918) 825-6677

Old Fashioned Day (May)
Chouteau
Amish festival with ethnic food booths, children's games, arts and crafts welcomes your leashed pet. There is even a police dog display.
(918) 476-8222
(918) 476-8311

Pecan Festival (June)
Okmulgee
The world's largest pecan baked item is concocted every year at this festival. Here you'll find arts and crafts, free entertainment, carnival rides, concessions galore, and more nuts (pecans) than you'd ever care to see.

Pecan Festival
(918) 756-6172

Chili Festival (October)
Okmulgee
Huge chili and brisket cook-off in downtown Okmulgee. The Hottest, Best-of Show, and other categories will take home trophies. All are invited to enter the contests. Bring Grandma's recipe and compete for prizes. Self-tasting kits (sounds kind of odd, doesn't it?) are available for you to sample all of the different chili entries.

Chili Festival
(918) 756-6172

Texas

Sights/Towns To See

Alpine
Woodward Agate Ranch
Red-plume, Pom-pom and other beautiful agates can be found on these 3,000 acres of excitement. Ranch experts help with tours and grading guidance. Jasper, feldspar, precious opal and pails full of gems can be extracted for a nominal fee. Dogs are treated with the respect they deserve here too! They are allowed to *run loose* (provided your dog is well behaved with both people and other dogs--if not--he's allowed on a leash)!!! There are also two creeks for your pal to swim in! Is everybody happy?!!

Woodward Agate Ranch
Highway 118
HC-65 Box 40
Alpine, TX 79830
(915) 364-2271

Apache Trading Post
Marfa Mystery Lights information, gemstone jewelry, West Texas handicrafts, shells, fossils, rocks, and the largest collection of maps of the **Big Bend** region can be found in this fun store. It is home to two Malteses, and welcomes your friendly dog to shop along with you.

Apache Trading Post
U.S. 90
Alpine, TX 79830
(915) 837-5506

Hotels/Motels
The Corner House   Amenities:G,R,T   Cost:**
801 E. Ave. E
Alpine, TX 79830
(915) 837-7161

Highland Inn   Amenities:G,R,T   Cost:**
1404 E. Hwy 90
Alpine, TX 79830
(915) 837-5811

Athens
Pet-friendly town allows pets in many places in this, the hardwood
country of Texas. "Hardwood" means that unlike all the desert and
scrub-pine places in Texas, this place has large trees and great fall
foliage. Home of the **New York Cheesecake** outlet - I'll bet you
thought that **New York Cheesecake** was made in the Northeast - you
can sample their wares in town and at local restaurants. While the
factory itself does not allow dogs inside, it is now on the central square
in Athens, so you could walk your pooch over and enjoy your
cheesecake outside. Lynn, of **Dunsavage Farms**, will gladly put you
and your pet up while in Athens. There is a lake at the farm that your
pet can swim in too!

Purtis State Recreation Area also allows pets in their 1,533 acre park
where there is camping, fishing, boating, picnicking and a playground.
Pets can't go in the water to swim, but they can go on the beach.
Purtis State Creek Recreation Area
Off U.S. 175
Athens, TX
(903) 425-2332

New York Cheesecake Outlet
Athens, TX
(903) 675-2281

Hotels/Motels
Dunsavage Farms   Amenities:G,R,T   Cost:**
Box 176
La Rue, TX 75770
(800) 440-2959

SOUTH-CENTRAL

The "Alamo"/Alamo Village
Brackettville
The movie set site of John Wayne's film, "The Alamo", it is claimed
that this set is a better way to see the Alamo than visiting the actual
place. (The real Alamo is in San Antonio.) Eighteen buildings and
countless films bring back Texas history as you enjoy country and
western shows, staged shoot-outs, and a typical old west atmosphere.
Eat a hearty lunch in the cantina-restaurant during your historic tour.
Films made here include; "Lonesome Dove", "Gunsmoke", "Bad
Girls", "Texas", and "Streets of Laredo", etc. Pets are welcome all
over the "town".

Alamo Village
RM 674
Brackettville, TX
(210) 563-2580

Texas Safari Wildlife Park
Clifton
Over 850 acres of plains, hills and natural canyons are home to 2,500
exotic animals. Your leashed pet is welcome in selective places, like
the simulated shootout that takes place on the summer weekends in the
frontier town replica. I immediately asked how the park animals felt
about a shootout every weekend. I was told that they don't mind...You
have to wonder...The drive-through safari also allows your pet, but
he/she must be leashed within the car at all times. The park animals are
tame and often hand-fed by patrons and it wouldn't do to have an
"incident", if you know what I mean.

Texas Safari Park
FM 3220
Clifton, TX 76634
(817) 675-3658

Hotels/Motels
The River's Bend B&B   Amenities: N/A   Cost: **
P.O. Box 228
Clifton, TX 76634
(817) 675-4936

Moscow Dinosaur Gardens
Moscow
Right on Highway 59, you can see life size replicas of dinosaurs along a 1,000 ft. path through the woods. They speak too! Hear the great smilodon's prehistoric growl as you pass by.

Dinosaur Gardens
U.S. 59
Moscow, TX
(409) 398-4565

McKinney Falls State Park
Austin
A beautiful waterfall, birds and mammals galore, and picnicking, swimming (not for Fido,though), camping (and RVs), hiking and just relaxing away from Austin proper await the weary traveler. Never seen an armadillo? You could see one here-they're all over the place!

McKinney Falls State Park
(512) 243- 1643

Austin
Enjoy the Victorian mansions in the Congress Avenue and Hyde Park sections downtown. Watch the bats emerge at dusk from under the Congress Avenue Bridge after your walking tour of the great homes. Canoe and hike with the pup in Zilker Park. Other neat parks are Enchanted Rock, Bastrop State Park, and Mckinney Falls. Go out on your own for a little while and enjoy the music and entertainment offered in many downtown locations (especially on Sixth Street).

Canoe Rental
(512) 478-3852

Bats
(512) 929-3600

Austin Parks & Recreation
(512) 477-7273

SOUTH-CENTRAL

Hotels/Motels
Doubletree Guest Suites   Amenities: S,R,T,G   Cost:***
303 West 15th St.
Austin, TX 78701
(512) 478-7000

Dog-Friendly Beaches
Lake Athens/North of LaRue
Port Aransas Beaches
Galveston Beaches/Galveston
Brazoria Beaches/South TX
South Padre Island Beaches
Corpus Christi Beaches

NORTH-CENTRAL

NORTH-CENTRAL

Iowa
Minnesota
Nebraska
North Dakota
South Dakota

Hotel Cost Codes (for average one-night stay)

*	$30-60/night
**	$61-100/night
***	$101-150/night
****	$151 and up/night
W	Hotel has weekly rates only

Note: costs may vary by season.

Hotel Amenity Codes

A	Airport nearby
H	Handicapped access
HS	Hair salon on premises
G	Golf within 10 miles
NS	Non-smoking rooms available
OB	Facility is on the beach
P	Playground on premises
R	Restaurant on premises
S	Swimming on premises
SA	Sauna on premises
SK	Skiing within 25 miles
T	Tennis within 10 miles

NORTH-CENTRAL

NORTH-CENTRAL
Iowa

Sights/Towns To See

Winterset
Ever find yourself wistful for the movie "Bridges of Madison County"?
You can relive every scene in this town where it was filmed. Drop in
at the Northside and sit on the stool Clint Eastwood sat on when his
character stopped in town. Check out the Corner Tavern where Clint
and Meryl Streep's character first danced. It's a friendly little place
(Francesca's home is just outside of town) where you can find peace
and relaxation.

Iowa Day Trips
(800) 345-4692

Hotels/Motels
The Village View   Amenities: N/A   Cost:**
711 East Hwy 92
Winterset, IA 50273

Comfort Inn   Amenities: G,H,R,S   Cost:**
5231 Fleur Dr.
Des Moines, IA 50321
(515) 287-3434

Ramada Limited   Amenities: A,H,R,S,NS   Cost:**
4684 NE 14th St.
Des Moines, IA 50313
(515) 265-5671

"Field of Dreams" Movie Site
Dyersville

The two farms where "Field of Dreams" was filmed have been enshrined (if you will) and you and the pet can visit. This Academy Award-nominated film is worth renting, especially if you're going to visit the site three miles north of Dyersville and stand in line for melted ice cream and souvenirs. My Ted likes vanilla.

28963 Lansing Rd.
Dyersville, IA 52040
(319) 875-8404

Effigy Mounds National Monument
Harpers Ferry

A wonderful Moonlight Hike displays eerie effigies and tracings of bears and birds on prehistoric Indian burial mounds dating from 500 B.C. Dogs are allowed at this outdoor site on a leash (though it seems to me to be an accident waiting to happen as Fifi mistakes the two thousand year old bird for a hydrant--oops!- and you are banned for life from any collection of artifacts dating before 1950). A great place. Be careful!

(319) 873-3491

Festivals/Happenings

Madison County Covered Bridge Festival (October)
Lovely foliage dominates this fall festival. Tours of the famous film sites and visits to the six historic covered bridges are part of the fun, food, music, and parades in this celebration.

Iowa City Farmer's Market
Iowa Festival of the Arts
Jazz Festival
Downtown Iowa City

All three activities welcome pets and are outside. This acceptance is related to the fact that almost all 23 Iowa City parks allow pets! Black Springs, Circle, and City Park, and Happy Hollow (Brown St.), or Willow Creek Park (Teg Drive) are but a few of those that are happy to accomodate your pet.

Jazz Festival
Iowa Arts Festival
325 E. Washington Street
(319) 337-9637

Farmer's Market
(319) 356-5110

Hotels/Motels

Comfort Inn of Coralville	Amenities: N/A	Cost:**

209 W. 9th St.
Coralville, IA 52241
(319) 351-8144

Tri-City KC Dog Show (September)
Fairgrounds
Davenport, IA

Contact:
MB-F Inc.
P.O. Box 22107
Greensboro, NC 27420
(800) 334-0813
(910) 379-9352

Art on the Fence
Cedar Rapids
This 30-year old festival welcomes walkers-by with pets. It is held every year outside 224 Crescent Street, at the Brucemore historical home. A gathering of mostly local artists, it is a summer highlight in Cedar Rapids. Brucemore can be rented, they tell me, for birthdays or weddings or just to allow you to feel for a moment like the wealthiest man in town who built it.

Art on the Fence
(319) 363-4942

NORTH-CENTRAL

Hotels/Motels
Days Inn   Amenities: N/A   Cost:**
3245 Southgate Pl. SW
Cedar Rapids, IA 52404
(319) 365-4339

Minnesota

Sights/Towns To See

The Spam Museum
Austin
Mess your dog's head up and come home smelling like canned luncheon meat. Just kidding, though this is a museum dedicated to those who helped make Spam what(?) it is today. See GI Janes as The Hormel Girls, the drum and bugle corps used to promote Hormel products. Replicas of rail cars shipping Spam, displays of how it was shipped, and comedian George Burns in a promotional ad, can all be found in this unusual attraction. Pets, unfortunately, are not allowed, but I felt compelled to include this one anyway.

The Spam Museum
Oak Park Mall
Austin, MN 55912
(507) 437-5611

Hotels/Motels
Rodeway Inn   Amenities: N/A   Cost:**
3303 Oakland Ave. W.
Austin, MN 55912
(507) 437-7774

Hennepin Parks
Minneapolis/St. Paul
25,000 acres of parks and reserve in and around the Twin Cities welcomes your dog on designated pet trails. Such trails can be found in Elm Creek Park in Osseo, Lake Sarah near Rockford, and Crow-Hassan Park near Rodgers. Other Hennepin parks will also welcome your pooch and can be determined upon arrival by contacting the Park System.

NORTH-CENTRAL

Hennepin Parks System
Minneapolis/St. Paul
(612) 559-9000
(612) 559-6719

Capitol City Trolley
View charming St. Paul from the old-fashioned Capitol City Trolley
with your best friend. They run year-round and are available for
chartered tours. Just a quarter buys you and Fido a fun ride back
through history. Small pets are preferred.
Capitol City Trolley
55E. 5th St.
Midwest Center, Suite 1340
St. Paul, MN 55101
(612) 223-5600

Cass Lake
Charming 600 acre lake stocked with wall-eye and muskie for
fishermen. Canoes, pontoon, paddle, motor, and row boats available.
Picnic, play, swim, fish, and relax at this peaceful attraction. Fido may
swim, but cannot use the beaches.

Hotels/Motels
Trees Resort   Amenities: S,SA,T   Cost:W
RR-2, Box 258
Cass Lake, MN 56633
(218) 335-2471
(800) 35-TREES

View Point Resort   Amenities:S,G   Cost:W
Little Wolf Lake
RR-3, Box 642
Cass Lake, MN 56633
(218) 335-6746

Nebraska

Sights/Towns To See

Avenue of Flags/4th of July Celebration
Auburn
More than 500 flags go up before each 4th of July to commemorate the veterans of war. Fireworks, barbeque and ice cream social are all events that you and your dog may attend outdoors.
Chamber of Commerce
1211 J Street
Auburn, NE 68305
(402) 274-3521

Hotels/Motels

Auburn Inn Motel	Amenities: N/A	Cost:**
US 75 North		
517 J Street		
Auburn, NE 68305		
(402) 274-3143		

Palmer House Motel	Amenities: N/A	Cost:**
Hwys 73/75 South		
1918 J Street		
Auburn, NE 68305		
(402) 274-3193		

Festivals/Happenings

Summer Fun Daze (June)
Burwell
Garfield county's answer to summer doldrums, the Summer Daze sponsors the 3-night D.C. Lynch carnival show with 15 rides and 10+ concessions. Burwell also holds a Barbeque and a Watermill game during the heat of July.

Chamber of Commerce
207 Grand
Burwell, NE 68823
(308) 346-5121

Hotels/Motels
Calamus River Lodge   Amenities: R   Cost:**
Calamus Lake Rd.
HC 79 Box 18A
Burwell, NE 68823
(308) 346-4331

Rodeo Inn   Amenities: S   Cost:**
Hwys 91 & 11
P.O. Box 475
Burwell, NE 68823-0475
(308) 346-4408

Jazz on the Green (June)
Omaha
Joslyn Art Museum hosts a variety of vocal and instrumental groups on
the Green in June. From 7 to 9 PM on a hot Thursday evening, you
and your best friend can wander on down to the best jazz in Douglas
County.

Joslyn Museum
2200 Dodge St.
Omaha, NE 68102
(402) 342-3300

Hotels/Motels
Clarion Hotel   Amenities: G,H,R,S   Cost:**
10909 M St.
Omaha, NE 68137
(402) 331-8220

NORTH-CENTRAL

Spring Fling (June)
Grand Island
Railroad Town and The Stuhr Museum host this dog-friendly fling complete with a 19th century melodrama,a band concert, arboretum tours and games for the kiddies. My favorite is the buffalo chip toss---bet ya can't eat just one. Just kidding.
3133 West Hwy. 34
Grand Island, NE 68801
(308) 385-5316

Hotels/Motels

Oak Grove Inn	Amenities: NS	Cost:**
3205 S. Locust Street		
Grand Island, NE 68801		
(308) 384-1333		
(800) 435-7144		

Conoco Motel	Amenities: NS,S,R	Cost:**
2107 West Second St.		
Grand Island, NE 68802		
(308) 384-2700		

Lazy V Motel	Amenities: S	Cost:**
2703 East Hwy 30		
Grand Island, NE 68801		

Old Mill Days (Summer)
Neligh
Dogs are welcome at this melange (mish-mash?) of midwestern entertainment. Mesmerizing in its magnitude, there are water fights, golf shoots, nature *runs* (I wonder how much of the delicate, umbelliferous flora one can perceive while off on a tear...), rubber ducky derby, scavenger hunts, sack races, tractor pulls, money races (I know *that* game!), turtle races, etc. Find anything you like? Don't worry, you will. They have everything!
419 Main St.
Neligh, NE 68756
(402) 887-4840

NORTH-CENTRAL

Hotels/Motels

DeLuxe Motel   Amenities: N/A   Cost:**
Hwy 275 East
P.O. Box 113
Neligh, NE 68756
(402) 887-4628

West Hillview Motel   Amenities: NS   Cost:**
West Hwy 275
Rt. 2 Box 43
Neligh, NE 68756
(402) 887-4186

North Dakota

Sights/Towns To See

Icelandic State Park
Cavalier /Wahalla
Camping, hiking, and lots of activities welcome your leashed pet here. There is the **Pioneer Machinery Show** (September), with old tractors and cars, pancake breakfast, flea market, church service, etc. The **Rendezvous Region Festival** (June) is a three-day encampment of traders, concessioners, campers, speakers, and musicians that all gather to trade and barter goods. Sounds interesting.

Hotels/Motels
Icelandic State Park Camping
(701) 265-4561

Cedar Inn   Amenities:R   Cost:**
Hwy 18 S.
Cavalier, ND
(701) 265-8341

Fort Stevenson State Park
Garrison
Surrounded by Lake Sakakawea, Fort Stevenson is a park rich with dog friendly activities. Watch the **CANDISC** (Cycling Around North Dakota In Sakakawea County) which is a bicycle fest, **Skydance Sakakawea** (a large kite-flying party), and **Fort Stevenson** military base which holds periodic re-enactments of military life in the 1800's. There is a **Triathalon** in August each year and your dog can swim in the lake! Lots of fun!

Hotels/Motels
Garrison Motel   Amenities: N/A   Cost:**
Hwy 37
Garrison, ND
(701) 463-2858

NORTH-CENTRAL

Jamestown

"Buffalo City" has the largest (60 ton) buffalo sculpture in the world! It is amazing to stand and view the beautiful scenery from the top of the hill on which the big ole boy stands. Friendship city (a large recreation complex) is host to the sculpture as well as to Frontier Village which welcomes your pet in the old fashioned dentist's office, barbershop and saloon. The buffalo stands watch in the eastern part of Frontier Village near where 2 dozen live buffalo roam the plains. It's a fun place to visit.

Festivals/Happenings

World's Largest Corn Maze

Fargo

Fargo grows and trims this three acre corn maze for people and pets to venture through and try their luck. Open from dawn to dusk in the summer, it is found on 124th Avenue.

World's Largest Corn Maze
2005 124th Ave. South
Fargo, ND
(701) 235-4261

Hotels/Motels
Comfort Inn   Amenities: G,H,R,S   Cost:**
3825 9th Ave. SW
Fargo, ND 58103
(701) 282-9596

Econo Lodge   Amenities: G,H,R,S   Cost:**
1401 35th St.
Fargo, ND 58103
(701) 232-3412

South Dakota

Sights/Towns To See

The Black Hills
The stunning "Dances with Wolves" with Kevin Costner was set in these stark and unforgiving hills. The Hills appear black because of the dark pines that cover them. Special sites include Devil's Tower in Wyoming (remember "Close Encounters of the Third Kind"?), the Badlands, and several interesting caves for the amateur spelunker. Many parks, caves and vendors at every site make for a busy and fun-filled visit. You may explore nearly all of the outdoor sites with your pet.

Mount Rushmore
Remember that exciting scene in Alfred Hitchcock's "North by Northwest" where Cary Grant and Melanie Griffith's mom, Tippi Hedren are being pursued across the face of this great monument? Although mostly studio-shot, it gives the feel of the vastness of the park (which is about 1500 acres) and the incredible skill of the sculptor of this bust of four of our Presidents. The rangers welcome controlled, leashed, and picked-up-after pets. There are wonderful interpretive tours about the carving of the monument by Gutzon Borglum, how the Presidents were chosen, etc.

I must confess, I figured out why Washington, Jefferson, and Lincoln were chosen, but I didn't know why Teddy Roosevelt was up there. Well, shame on me. It turns out that he was one of the most forward thinking Presidents we've ever had. He supported and encouraged land conservation long before it was a popular issue.

Movies, tours and special programs are available at this attraction which gets 20,000 people a day in the summer. My favorite is the evening program which starts with a movie at dusk, then the National Anthem is played and the monument is proudly lit against the night sky. Kinda gives you goosebumps just thinking about it.

NORTH-CENTRAL

Mt. Rushmore
(605) 574-2523

Hotels/Motels
Brookside Motel   Amenities: N/A   Cost: **
603 Reed St.
P.O. Box 137
Keystone, SD 57751
(800) 551-9381
(605)666-4496

Comfort Inn   Amenities: G,H,R,S,T   Cost: **
1550 N. LaCrosse
Rapid City, SD 57701
(605) 348-2221

Wind Cave National Park
Hot Springs
The park welcomes your pet on leash on all trails except the hiking trails and the 37 miles of underground caves. There are 28,000 acres to explore!

Wind Cave National Park
(605) 745-4600

Crystal Cave Park
Rapid City
The cave is several hundred feet deep with stairs leading into it. There is a great spelunking opportunity here, but Fido may not go below. The friendly folks here say that they'll watch your dog for you in the pet-friendly gift shop while you explore. The hound is allowed on the grounds too.

Cyrstal Cave
(605) 342-8008

The Corn Palace
Mitchell
Actually the large Mitchell Civic Auditorium, it is decorated inside with permanent ornamentation made of corn and other grains. It has historical significance to the town and the history is traced in pictures and drawings inside. Outside each fall, the townsfolk decorate it with a corn or grain theme for visitors.

The Corn Palace
(605) 996-7311

Pet-Friendly Campgrounds

Happy Holiday Campground/Rapid City
Lazy 'J' Campground/Rapid City
Grace Coolidge @ Custer State Park/Custer

NORTH-CENTRAL

SOUTHWEST

SOUTHWEST

SOUTHWEST

Arizona
California
Colorado
Nevada
New Mexico
Utah

Hotel Cost Codes (for average one-night stay)

*	$30-60/night
**	$61-100/night
***	$101-150/night
****	$151 and up/night
W	Hotel has weekly rates only

Note: costs may vary by season.

Hotel Amenity Codes

A	Airport nearby
H	Handicapped access
HS	Hair salon on premises
G	Golf within 10 miles
NS	Non-smoking rooms available
OB	Facility is on the beach
P	Playground on premises
R	Restaurant on premises
S	Swimming on premises
SA	Sauna on premises
SK	Skiing within 25 miles
T	Tennis within 10 miles

SOUTHWEST

SOUTHWEST
Arizona

Sights/Towns To See

Phoenix/Scottsdale
Hike, relax and enjoy the comforts of civilized, dog-friendly Scottsdale and Phoenix. Scottsdale has dozens of art galleries, boutiques, bookstores, and antique dealers. Phoenix has great parks to hike with your friend, such as North Mountain in the center of Phoenix. Other parks include Papago Park, Encanto Park and Squaw Peak Park. Check out festivals there such as hot air-ballooning, musical, and arts & crafts events.

Hotels/Motels
Inn at the Citadel   Amenities:N/A   Cost:****
8700 E. Pinnacle Peak Rd.
Scottsdale, AZ 85255
(602) 585-6133, (800) 927-8367

Wyndham Garden Hotel   Amenities:N/A   Cost:***
2641 W. Union Hills
Phoenix, AZ 85027
(602) 978-2222

Festivals/Happenings

Annual Fiddle Contest (February)
Tucson
City-wide competition for the best fiddlers in each of several categories. Youth, Children, Adults, Bluegrass and other categories can be heard at this annual event.

Civics Orchestra Concert (April)
Tucson
Traditional Sousa-type happy, marching music fills the air at this pet-friendly concert.

Orts Dance Concert (August)
10th Street Dance Works (September)
Tucson
A modern dance company creates new choreography to accompany their new music; or do they create the dance and then compose? You'll have to find out at these dog-friendly events.

Music Under The Stars (June)
Tucson
The Tucson Pops Orchsetra presents a romantic concert for you, your special friend, and another special friend (?). Or just for you! This is the best way to listen to lovely strains of classical music...

Jazz Sunday / Blues Festival (October)
Tucson
Both are exciting Reid Park events in a dog-friendly town and a dog-friendly park. Bring your own brunch or dinner to either concert and enjoy!

Reid Park
Tucson, AZ
(520) 791-4079

Arizona Symphonic Winds (June)
Tucson
Classical compositions tickle the ear with familiarity as this wonderful orchestra shares their talent in bucolic Udall Park.

Udall Park
Tucson, AZ
(520) 791-4079

Hotels/Motels

Red Roof Inn   Amenities: N/A   Cost:**
3700 E. Irvington Rd.
Tucson, AZ 85714
(602) 571-1400

Radisson Suite Tuscon   Amenities: N/A   Cost:***
6555 E. Speedway Blvd.
Tuscon, AZ 85710
(602) 721-7100

Annual Sweet Onion Festival (June)
Rock Springs
Educational booths, food, seeds, fresh veggies, recipes, contests and
competitions for the biggest, best, sweetest onions. Lots of fun for you
and the hound...
Annual Sweet Onion Festival
Rock Springs, AZ
(602) 465-9256

Norwest Climb The Mountain, Conquer Cancer (February)
Phoenix
South Mountain Park hosts this annual event to support The American
Cancer Society's lifesaving programs. Good food, exhilarating walk
up the mountain and leisurely stroll down, prizes and t-shirts for
participants make this a fun day. Fido is, of course, welcome.
Climb The Mountain
(602) 553-7129
(602) 919-4011

Night Lights - Light A Way To A Cure
Scottsdale
The American Cancer Society hosts this fun event at Eldorado Park
that includes competitive 5K and 10K runs, a family fitness walk, and a
moving Lights of Hope Ceremony at the end. Complimentary
beverages are served in the nightime festival area.
Night Lights
(602) 553-7129

California

Sights/Towns To See

Carmel/Monterey

Picturesque Carmel village is purposefully quaint; no neon signs, no stop lights, and lovely architecture is the order of the day. A former artist's colony, Carmel boasts great galleries, shops, boutiques, and scenery. And if you're a movie fan, Clint Eastwood ,"The Enforcer", was mayor here for several years.

Ride the most photographed highway in the West, Route 1, down the coast to see the Redwoods and Big Sur. Garland Ranch Park allows leashed pets, and the view is magnificent as you hike along the Carmel River and up the mountains. Carmel Beach and the little beach known as Delmar Beach allow UNLEASHED(!) pets to "gyre and gimble in the wabe(s)" and the pearly white sand. Wonderful Doris Day has a great pet friendly inn right here in Carmel, The Cypress Inn.

Cypress Inn
Carmel·By·The·Sea, California

The helpful concierge of the Cypress Inn has lists of pet-friendly activities as well as restaurants. Le Coq D'or, Cafe Berlin, Casanova, The Avenue, Anton & Michael, Cafe Gringo, Prima Cafe 6th Avenue Grill, Le Bistro, Paolinas, Little Pizza Heaven, Plaza Cafe & Grill and Cafe Stravaganza are some of the best pet-friendly restaurants in the area.

Towns to visit: Carmel, Monterey, Seaside, Pacific Grove

Carmel Chamber of Commerce
(408) 624-2522

Hotels/Motels
The Cypress Inn   Amenities: NS   Cost:***
7th Ave. & Lincoln
Carmel, CA 93921
(800) 443-7443

(Mailing address)
P.O. Box "Y"
Carmel, CA 93921

San Francisco
Take the trolleys with your well-behaved or small pet (a muzzle may still be required; if so, Ted and I will walk, thank you). Explore the city of sourdough bread, steep streets and Fisherman's Wharf. The arts are alive in San Francisco, and the temperature is always just right. The Palace of Fine Arts is a lovely place to enjoy Greek architecture and relax outside with your pet.

Take a hike on the Golden Gate Bridge; see Angel Island, Alcatraz, and the waterfront downtown, all from the bridge. Visit Golden Gate Park, Alta Plaza Park, Bernal Heights Park, Buena Vista Park, and Corona Heights Park (all dog friendly and some leash-free!). Boat on Stow Lake with Fido. He can swim off Baker or Ocean beaches.

SOUTHWEST

See the sea lions off Pier 39 and cruise the bay with the Red and White
Fleet.   Relive "Star Trek IV" and "The Enforcer" while in San
Francisco.

Hotels/Motels
Hilton & Towers   Amenities: R   Cost: ***
333 O'Farrell Sty.
San Francisco, CA
(415) 771-1400

Marriott Fisherman's Wharf   Amenities: R   Cost: ***
San Francisco, CA
(415) 775-7555

Beresford Arms   Amenities: R   Cost: **
San Francisco
(800) 533-6533

Mansions Hotel   Amenities: R   Cost: ***
San Francisco
(415) 929-9444

Four Seasons Clift   Amenities: R   Cost: ****
San Francisco
(415) 775-4700

Haus Kleebauer B&B   Amenities: R   Cost: **
San Francisco
(415) 821-3866

Rodeway Inn   Amenities: R   Cost: ***
San Francisco
(415) 673-0691

The Hollywood Sign
Hollywood Hills
Take a picture of you and the pooch in Hollywood. Beachwood Drive
leads you to Hollyridge Drive. Walk up Hollyridge Drive onto the Mt.
Lee Trail. The trail takes you to the Hollywood sign. Go up the hill,

bear left, and look for the sign; the trail is about three miles long. "Lethal Weapon" was made in the Hollywood Hills and environs.

The Hollywood Sign
(213) 665-5188

The Wheel Inn & Restaurant
Cabazon
Ah! The site of the uniquely funny, "Peewee's Big Adventure", this is where you can find (and go into) the two giant dinosaurs that Peewee visited. You enter the brontosaurus through the tail and there's a gift shop in the head! I think the truck stop is the site of the biker scene as well. I don't think the pooch is welcome in the gift shop, but you can walk around and get take-out for both of you.

Wheel Inn & Restaurant
50-900 Seminole Drive
Cabazon, CA 92230
(909) 849-7012

Canine Camp of the Redwoods
Herding, agility, obedience are all part of this fun-filled camp for dogs. See the magnificent Redwoods and both of you can swim at a dog friendly beach. "Return of the Jedi" was made in the Redwood forests.

Carole Pitlock
Canine Camp of the Redwoods
204 Celia Ave.
Boulder Creek, CA 95006
(408) 338-1130

<u>**Festivals/Happenings**</u>

Mozart Festival (July)
San Luis Obispo
Much of this extravaganza takes place at The Mission in San Luis Obispo. While this area is not open to pets, many others are. In nearby Chapel Hill, chamber concerts are free and open to the public. Hear groups like the Festival Baroque ensemble fill the mountains with song.

SOUTHWEST

Pets are welcome here. A fortepiano concert is often the order of the day at the pet-friendly winery, Maison Deutz, during part of this two-week long festival. And visit the incredible seaside Chapman Estate where, for one day, the owner donates his home to the festival so that any and all (well-behaved pets too!) may come to the "Salute To Mozart".

Annual Festival of Whales (March)
Dana Point
What's cool about whale watching on the West coast is that you can do it while still on shore. Here in the East we have to boat 25 or so miles out before we see anything! Observe the gray whale migration and enjoy festivities such as an art show, great food, parade, and Fido's favorite, the Animal Wag-a-thon.

Festival of Whales
(800) 290-DANA
(714) 496-1555

Perseid Meteor Shower Festival (August)
Lake Arrowhead
This space and astronomy festival, in one of the best places to observe this yearly event, welcomes your pet. There's nothing more spectacular than watching a sky full of meteors shooting towards you. Any other night of the year you might casually see one. At this time you can see dozens with the unaided eye! While this event is only one night, the Perseids last for 3-4 nights, so you can observe them after this on your own.

Perseid Meteor Shower Festival
(909) 336-1699

California Dry Bean Festival (August)
Tracy
Headline bands help the town of Tracy celebrate their important crop-dry beans. Now that we know we should eat more beans for all the benefits they offer in terms of fiber and protein, I'm sure you'll all want to be there and take a few home with you! There are celebrity

chef demonstrations, a classic car show, arts and crafts, and much more!

Dry Bean Festival
(209) 835-2131

Basset Hound Picnic (Summer)
Arcadia
Longest ears, best trick and howling competitions are just some of the entertaining events promised at this event in Arcadia Park. A Rescue Dog Parade, Costume contests, and adorable basset hounds available for adoption or foster care while they await adoption. Basset hound owners must check this out! Owners of other breeds will have a great time as well!

Basset Hound Picnic
Arcadia, CA
(805) 584-1496

Hotels/Motels
Hampton Inn   Amenities: G   Cost:**
311 E. Huntington Dr.
Arcadia, CA 91006
(818) 574-5600

Nisei Week Japanese Festival (August)
Los Angeles
Kanichiwa. Down in Little Tokyo your pet is welcome to take part in the week-long festival celebrating all things Japanese. There is a parade, folk dancing, a carnival, arts and crafts, music and all kinds of exhibits.
Japanese Festival
(213) 687-7193

African Marketplace and Cultural Faire (August)
Los Angeles
Ten acre global village runs for weeks at Rancho Cienega and features hundreds of arts and crafts kiosks encompassing more than 40 cultures

SOUTHWEST

and 70 countries. Soccer matches, entertainment, children's games, great food, and the African Business Expo.

African Marketplace
(213) 237-1540
(213) 734-1164

Black Bart Festival (June)
Cloverdale
Amateur wine contest (no professional winos,...er, whiners...uh, wine makers allowed), Dressed-up Pets Parade, period fashion show, ram sale, and sheep dog trials fill the day with pet-friendly excitement.

Black Bart Festival
(707) 894-4470

Sonoma-Marin Fair (June)
Petaluma
Typical county fair with extras such as an Ugly Dog contest (again only for secure dogs!), Chili Cook-off, llamas and farm animals for petting, and many kiosks.

Sonoma-Marin County Fair
(707) 763-0931

Rocklin Jubilee (June)
Rocklin
Annual Independence Day celebration with 5K and 10K runs as well as a Pet Show, craft and food fair, entertainment and fireworks.

Rocklin Jubilee
(916) 632-4100

Monterey Wine Makers Celebration (August)
Monterey
Over twenty-five of the finest wineries in Monterey County participate in this annual event that includes entertainment, good food, great wine, and wine displays. Remember, Fido is always underage! The wine is

SOUTHWEST

for you! Patronize this and other pet-friendly events to show them it means a lot to have your best friend with you!

Monterey Wine Makers Celebration
(408) 375-9400
(408) 655-0354

Old Port Redondo Days
Redondo Beach
Pie-baking contest, historical society picnic and fireworks, sea music, dancing, old-time crafts, and a Pet Parade make this a fun fest.

Old Port Redondo Days
(800) 282-0333

Camarillo Fiesta (October)
Camarillo
Ethnic arts and crafts, foods and parade. A Blessing of the Animals is also part of this event. Look for other Blessings of the Animals in October because this is the time of year that St. Francis is remembered for his goodness to the animals.

Camarillo Fiesta
(805) 388-5307

Feast of Lanterns/Children's Pet Parade (July)
Caledonia Park
Pacific Grove, CA
(408) 372-7625

American Family Pet Expo (April)
Fairplex
Pomona,CA
(818) 447-2222

Dog Parks
Ohlone Dog Park/ Berkeley
The Dog Park/ Santa Clara
Bernal Heights/San Francisco

SOUTHWEST

Remington Dog Park/ Sausalito
Mission Trails Park/San Diego
Larkspur's Canine Companions/ Sunnyvale
Las Palmas Dog Park/ Sunnyvale
Field of Dogs/ San Raphael
Dominguez Park/ Redondo Beach
Long Beach Recreation Park/ Long Beach
Bark Park/ Laguna Beach

Dog Friendly Beaches
Santa Cruz/ Rio Del Mar
Santa Cruz/ Seabright
Carmel Beach/Carmel
Delmar Beach/Carmel
Gold Bluffs Beach/Northern CA
Sinkyone/Northern CA
Mendocino Beaches/Mendocino
Bay Area Beaches/ SF
Ocean Beach/SF
Muir Beach/SF
Rodeo Beach/SF
Baker Beach/SF
Crissy Field/SF
Rio del Mar/Santa Cruz
Pismo Dunes/Southern CA
Seaside/Ventura
Marina/Ventura
Thornhill Broome Beach/Point Mugu
Leo Carrillo State Beach/Southern CA

Colorado

Sights/Towns To See

Telluride
Where else can you get an 18 hole golf course, indoor rock climbing, mountain biking, tennis, racquetball, nutritional counseling, a resort town that Ski Magazine rated in the top 5 places to ski, a spa rated second in the U.S. (only to the Canyon ranches), the view used in the Coors commercials and people that love your dog enough to allow him in any room in the hotel? Telluride, that's where. The Peaks is the place to stay; although high season rates are high, it is well worth it. All guests get full use of the 44 room spa and aerobics classes, weight training and all the other fun stuff like the water slide and pool. In town you can rent a jeep and go off and explore a deserted mining town or enjoy Shakespeare in the Park with your pooch. Beat that!

Hotels/Motels
The Peaks   Amenities: R,S,T,G,etc.   Cost: ****
136 Country Club Drive
P.O. Box 2702
Telluride, CO 81435
(800) 789-2220

Aspen
The place to see or be seen, Aspen plays host to the rich and famous each ski season. If you want to avoid the maddening crowds, how about a cross-country tour? Ski Independence Pass Road, Owl Creek corridor, and other spots that have cross-country trails. Or ski downhill for part of the day and entertain your pooch for the rest. The best of both worlds! Hotel Jerome is a great place to relax and unwind with lots of amenities! Cresthaus is a 10 minute walk from downtown Aspen.

Ski Info
(800) 290-1325

Aspen Info
(303) 925-1940

Hotels/Motels
Hotel Jerome   Amenities: S,R,T   Cost:***
330 East Main St.
Aspen, CO 81611
(970) 920-1000

Cresthaus Lodge   Amenities: S,SA   Cost: ***
1301 East Cooper
Aspen, CO 81611
(970) 925-7081

Limelite Lodge   Amenities: N/A   Cost:***
228 East Cooper
Aspen, CO 81611
(970) 925-3025

Leadville
On my list of favorite movies is "The Unsinkable Molly Brown". Scenes from the movie start in Leadville and, after a look at Europe, return to Denver. I have always loved what I knew to be a fun, fictional story, and got a real shock when I found out that Molly and JJ Brown actually did exist! Not only that, but the story is completely true! You can tour their home in Denver and the mine they discovered here in Leadville. It's an oldie but a goodie featuring the lovely Debbie Reynolds, and if you haven't seen it and are planning a Colorado tour, you must rent the video.

There are at least three restaurants with outdoor seating in town that occasionally allow pet owners to dine avec la pooch; Wild Bill's, High Country, Tabor Coffee House, and the local pizzeria. There are lots of outdoor activities (Ski Cooper), museums, and shopping. It is a great destination for budget minded people as well because everything is reasonably priced.

Hotels/Motels
Silver King   Amenities: SK,R   Cost: **
2020 N. Popular
Leadville, CO 80461
(800) 871-2610

Timberline/ Mt. Peaks   Amenities: SK   Cost: **
216 Harrison Ave.
Leadville, CO
(800) 352-1876

Other Hotels
The Bel Air
(719) 486-0881

The Alps
(800) 818-2577

Mt. Albert
(801) 381-4433

Phoenix Gold Mine
Idaho Springs
Tour the mine and chisel or pan for your own gold with the dog. There
is lots of room and people may pan almost anywhere on the property.
There is picnicking on the property as well. The owner says he prefers
controlled dogs that are used to other people.

Phoenix Gold Mine
Trail Creek Rd.
P.O. Box 751
Idaho Springs, CO 80452
(303) 567-0422

Miramont Castle
Tour the lovely first floor miniature houses and dolls patterned after
different cities like London. Four floors of period pieces from the
1890's have manequins in appropriate attire in the rooms and there is a

train museum on the grounds as well. Small pets are allowed inside, large ones can tour the gardens outside (but not the house).

Miramont Castle
Capitol Hill Ave.
Manitou Springs, CO 80829
(719) 685-1011

Celestial Seasonings
Boulder
Dogs are allowed outside at the picnic tables in the summer; try not to go when it's too hot because there is little shade out front. Sit by the Tea Shop and the Cafe with your hound. The tour must exclude him for health reasons, but there are atill ways to have fun. Browse the gift shop and do your holiday chores early - everybody loves tea!

Celestial Seasonings
4600 Sleepytime Drive
Boulder, CO 80301
(303) 581-1250

Great Sand Dunes National Monument
Mosca
Sand dunes are lots of fun to roll and slide around in, but what if formally organized activities for the dunes included downhill and cross-country skiing?!! Only in the summer! (Remember the sensitive paws on hot sand and go early or late in the day.) Only in Colorado!

This great mountainous hill of sand also has hiking, bird watching, and just admiring the view on its list of things to do with your best friend. Concerned about erosion, I asked the park representative if the sand will disappear someday with all this activity. "No way," she said with a laugh, "It blows right back up daily!" You can find this special place high in the San Luis Valley, next to the Sangre de Cristo Mountains.

Great Sand Dunes National Monument
11500 Highway 50
Mosca, CO 81146
(719) 378-2312

SOUTHWEST

Festivals/Happenings

Octoberfest (September)
Winterfest (December)
Outdoor Concerts (Summer)
Denver
All of these can be found in pet-friendly Larimer Square in downtown Denver. There are seven outdoor restaurants with seating that occasionally allows pets and lots of shopping, history, and carriage rides through town.

Larimer Square
1429 Larimer Street
Denver, CO 80202
(303) 534-2367

Animal Fair
Douglas County Fair Grounds
Castle Rock, CO
(800) 243-2187, (303) 979-6473

Winterskol Parade
Aspen
Dogs actually march in this parade and there is a fashion show before the parade. Lots of storeowners have treats for dogs that visit regularly.

Aspen Info
(303) 925-1940

Nevada

Sights/Towns To See

Ghost Towns
Virginia City
Austin
Pioche
Eureka
Tonopah
Goldfield
Belmont
Berlin
Rhyolite
Unionville

These towns are in different states of repair; Rhyolite, for example, is very photogenic and completely deserted, but Tonopah is a living ghost town that celebrates Jim Butler Days (mining sports events) every year. Pioche was known as the toughest town in Nevada and at one point accounted for 60% of all homocides in the state. Unionville is one of the most attractive of the ghost towns with ruins that stretch for almost three miles. The Nevada Chamber Of Commerce will gladly give you a guide to these towns.

Nevada's Living Ghost Towns (a publication)
Nevada Magazine
Capitol Complex
Carson City, NV 89710
(702) 687-5416

Festivals/Happenings

Camp Winnaribbun
Lake Tahoe camp offers agility, obedience, tracking, hiking, swimming, and fun for you and your pet.

SOUTHWEST

Camp Winnaribbun
P.O. Box 50300
Reno, NV 89513
(702) 747-1561

International Pet Expo
Sands Convention Center
Las Vegas, NV
(818) 447-2222

Hotels/Motels
Rodeway Inn   Amenities: G,H,R,T,SA   Cost: **
2050 Market St.
Reno, NV 89502
(702) 786-2500

Howard Johnson Lodge   Amenities: R,S,NS   Cost: *
1322 Fremont St.
Las Vegas, NV 89101
(702) 385-1150

Pet Friendly State Parks
Death Valley National Park
Beatty, NV
(619) 786-2331

Beaver Dam State Park
Caliente, NV
(702) 728-4467

Berlin-Ichthyosaur State Park
Gabbs, NV
(702) 964-2440

Cathedral Gorge State Park
Panaca, NV
(702) 728-4467

SOUTHWEST

Echo Canyon / Spring Valley State Parks
Pioche, NV
(702) 962-5103
(702) 962-5102

Campgrounds/RV Parks (All of these have both)
Once again, this is just a sampling. Many of these hundreds of parks allow pets. Check with the Nevada Tourism Board for other areas if you need them.

Pioneer Territory
R Place
Hwy 93, HCR 61
Box 28B
Hiko, NV 89017
(702) 725-3545

Bailey's Hot Springs
Hwy 95
Beatty, NV 89003
(702) 553-2395

Burro Inn
Hwy 95
Beatty, NV 89003
(702) 553-2225
(800) 843-2078

Space Station RV Park
Hwy 95
Beatty, NV 89003
(702) 533-9039

Agua Caliente
Hwy 93
Caliente, NV 89008
(702) 725-3114

SOUTHWEST

Young's RV Park
Hwy 93
Caliente, NV 89008
(702) 726-3418

Reno-Tahoe Territory
Camp'N Town
2438 N. Carson St.
Carson City, NV 89706
(702) 883-1123
(800) 872-1123

Comstock Country RV Resort
5400 N. Carson St.
Carson City, NV 89701
(702) 882-2445

Pony Express Territory
Austin RV Park
Hwy 50
Austin, NV 89310
(702) 964-2393

The Y
Hwy 50 & SR 487
Baker, NV 89311
(702) 234-7223

Whispering Elms RV Park
State Hwy 487
Baker, NV 89311
(702) 234-7343

Cowboy Country
Denio Junction
P.O. Box 7035
Denio, NV 89404
(702) 941-0371

SOUTHWEST

Royal Peacock Opal
P.O. Box 55
Virgin Valley
Denio, NV 89404
(702) 941-0374

Rydon Campground
I-80
P.O. Box 1656
Elko, NV 90801
(702) 738-3448

Hidden Valley Guest & RV Resort
I-80
P.O. Box 1454
Elko, NV 90801
(702) 738-2347

New Mexico

Festivals/Happenings

New Mexico State Fair (September)
Albuquerque
A 17-day festival of all that is good about New Mexico, nightly country-western music, both Spanish and Indian restoration villages set up for viewing, a large carnival with rides, and other attractions. There is a rodeo, but skip it if you can; I never recommend watching them as rodeos can be cruel for the animals involved. Enjoy the music, food and other festivities.

New Mexico State Fair
Albuquerque, NM
(800) 284-2282

Hotels/Motels
Comfort Inn   Amenities: G,R,SK   Cost:*
13031 Central Ave.
Albuquerque, NM 87123
(505) 294-1800

Econo Lodge   Amenities: H,R,T,SA,SK   Cost:*
13211 Central Ave. NE
Albuquerque, NM 87123
(505) 292-7600

Carlsbad Caverns Bat Flight Breakfast (August)
In August the bats can be seen returning in the morning from their night of foraging for food. The sight of thousands of bats streaming in formation from miles away is incredible, and the caverns have created this sit-down breakfast for you to enjoy while watching their return. What about dogs? Well, if you bring your pet, you must stay at the edge of the amphitheater (which sits at the mouth of the cave) and not enter the cave.

SOUTHWEST

You may bring your own breakfast and stand there with your dog and marvel at the sight. (Don't forget the *scorpions* if you choose to sit down). If you want to partake of that which is served in the amphitheater, then Fido can wait for you in the kennel on site or at your pet friendly hotel. A caveat; the person I spoke with about bringing my dog said that dog's ears are sensitive to the bats high pitched sound and if you own a barker, you may want to leave him in his air-conditioned room at the hotel.

Carlsbad Caverns
(800) 221-1224
(505) 785-2232
(505) 887-6516

Hotels/Motels
Rodeway Inn   Amenities: S,R,T,SA   Cost:*
3804 National Parks Hwy.
Carlsbad, NM 88220
(505) 887-5535

Quality Inn   Amenities: R,G,H   Cost:**
3706 National Parks Hwy.
Carlsbad, NM 88220
(505) 887-2861

The Hatch Chile Festival
Taste all kinds of dishes made from the native red and green peppers. Enjoy mariachi bands and a fiddlers contest. (Do not offer chiles to your dog for any reason. Give your pet his normal food before you go so he/she won't be hungry at the festival.) Purchase one of the beautiful *ristras* necklaces made out of chiles or baskets of selected chiles from the local harvest.

Hatch Chile Festival
(505) 267-5050

Utah

Sights/Towns To See

Great Salt Lake
Antelope Island is a must visit as part of the 28,000 acres that make up the Great Salt Lake area. Pets are allowed in the park, but may be restricted from some of the festivals, like the Antelope Island by Moonlight Bike Ride which goes from 10 P.M. to 2 A.M. When asked about the timing of the ride, the answer was less romantic than I expected; that it's just too hot in the daylight hours to do such a thing. Remember that when thinking of bringing your pet; take him in the early or very late hours of the day. The Bonneville Salt Flats where auto testing and racing can be found are also a part of the Salt Lake area. See the Hot Salt One, Test Week, and the World Speed Finals at the Flats.

Great Salt Lake
(801) 773-2941
Bonneville Salt Flats
(801) 533-9176

Hotels/Motels

Hojo Inn   Amenities: H,R,S,NS   Cost: *
1167 S. Main
Brigham City, UT 84032
(801) 723-8511

Econo Lodge   Amenities: G,H,R,T,SK   Cost: *
715 W. North Temple
Salt Lake City, UT 84116
(801) 363-0062

Ramada Inn Downtown   Amenities: A,H,R,S,NS,SK   Cost: **
230 West 600 South
Salt Lake City, UT 84101
(801) 364-5200

Moab District/East Central and Southeastern Utah
The San Rafael Swell in Emery County is an oval shaped uplift well known to geologists. They have called it the Red Amphitheater for many years for its odd shape; many other geological oddities can be found there. Desolation Canyon and Labyrinthe Canyon in the Green River area allow pets, but there are many of these parks that do not. Two reasons are the extreme heat and the difficult climbs for pets.

Moab District Main Office
82 E. Dogwood
Moab, UT 84532
(801) 259-6111
Field Office - (801) 636-3600

Hotels/Motels

Comfort Suites	Amenities: G,H,R,S	Cost**
800 S. Main St.		
Moab, UT 84532		
(801) 259-5252		

Ramada Inn	Amenities: G,H,R,S,T,NS	Cost*
182 S. Main St.		
Moab, UT 83532		
(801) 259-7141		

Festivals/Happenings

Free State Park Day (June)
All state parks in Utah participate in this day where no admission is charged for any service in the parks. Parks involved that allow dogs include; Bear Lake, Willard Bay, East Canyon, Jordanelle, Deer Creek, Utah Lake, Starvation, Steinaker, Red Fleet, Scofield and Quail Creek. The park rangers do not like the dogs on the beaches or in the water, but everywhere else is fine.

Free State Park Day (801) 538-7221
U.S. Forest Service
(800) 280-2267
(801) 524-5030

SOUTHWEST

Huntsman World Senior Games
St. George

Over 16 separate events including road racing, volleyball, soccer, and cycling take place in St. George in the fall. Gold, silver, and bronze medals are given out in each event. You must be 50 or older to participate, but all are welcome to watch with their pooches. There are both social tennis and social golf events at which there is prize money at stake.

Huntsman World Senior Games
82 W. 700 S.
St. George, UT 84770
(801) 674-0550

Hotels/Motels

Travelodge East	Amenities: R	Cost**
175 N. 1000 East St.		
St. George, UT 84770		
(801) 673-4621		

Payson Scottish Festival
Payson

All the wonderful things you'd expect at a Scottish Festival, and you can bring your dog too! The traditional caber toss where a very strong, kilt-clad clansman hoists a tree trunk and throws it so that it lands upside down is a highlight of the day. Piping and drumming competitions (that take me back to childhood Scottish games) fill the grounds with nostalgic bagpipe sounds while highland dancers and clan vendors with spectacular plaid and silver wares share their insights and their amazing love of dogs. It seems that to be a true Scot, you must have a love of dogs. Cool.

Payson Scottish Festival
493 S. 100 E.
Payson, UT 84651
(801) 465-2933

Hotels/Motels
Comfort Inn
1555 Canyon Rd.
Provo, UT 84604
(801) 374-6020

Amenities: G,H,R,S,SK   Cost: **

NORTHWEST

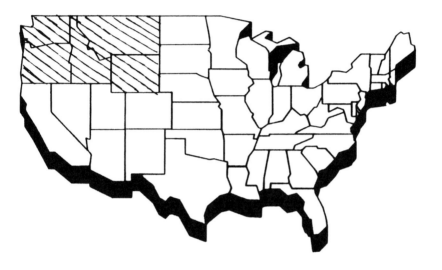

NORTHWEST

NORTHWEST

Idaho
Montana
Oregon
Washington
Wyoming

Hotel Cost Codes (for average one-night stay)

*	$30-60/night
**	$61-100/night
***	$101-150/night
****	$151 and up/night
W	Hotel has weekly rates only

Note: costs may vary by season.

Hotel Amenity Codes

A	Airport nearby
H	Handicapped access
HS	Hair salon on premises
G	Golf within 10 miles
NS	Non-smoking rooms available
OB	Facility is on the beach
P	Playground on premises
R	Restaurant on premises
S	Swimming on premises
SA	Sauna on premises
SK	Skiing within 25 miles
T	Tennis within 10 miles

NORTHWEST

NORTHWEST
Idaho

Sights/Towns To See

Emerald Creek
Got a minute? Got a bucket? You're in for the unique experience of mining your own gems! There is only one place in the world besides India where you can find star garnets of a deep purple color, here in Emerald Creek. You'll need a US Forest Service permit to do this, but it is easy to get and well worth it. Get up to a pound of gems per visit!

Emerald Creek
(208) 666-6000

Hotels/Motels
Comfort Inn   Amenities: N/A   Cost**
280 W. Appleway
Coeur D'Alene, ID 83814
(208) 765-5500

Spokane Bed & Breakfast   Amenities: N/A   Cost**
Reservation Service
E. 627 25th Ave.
Spokane, WA 99203
(509) 624-3776

Ketchum
Home of U.S. skier Pikabo Street, Ketchum plays host to many winter frolickers at nearby Sun Valley at the edge of the Smokey Mountains. Sun Valley was the first ski resort in the US. Ski Bald Mountain while your pet relaxes at pet-friendly River Street Inn, which welcomes pets of all kinds and has great views and pancake breakfasts. River Inn also boasts a Japanese soaking tub in each room and a nearby atheletic club.

Hotels/Motels
The River Street Inn   Amenities: R,SA   Cost: *
100 Rivers Street West
Ketchum, ID 83340
(208) 726-3611

Clarion Inn   Amenities: G,R,SK   Cost: **
600 Main Street
Ketchum, ID 83340
(208) 726-5900

Spencer Opal Mine
Several years ago on a trip to Hong Kong we stopped in the wonderful Jade Market behind Nathan Road, an informal but daily gathering of vendors of all sorts of precious and semi-precious gems. They poured their wares provacatively out into dark velvet tablecloths. It was incredible! To make a long story short, I first saw really large opals at this market, piles and piles of stones with beautiful green, purple red and blue colors glowing beneath that milky sheath. Ever since I have wanted to see such a thing again. Now I can, and so can you! And so can your pooch (provided he's leashed). Spencer Opal Mine in southeast Idaho allows you to dig for your own opals! They also have rough opals, half rough, and finished jewelry for your enjoyment and purchase. Happy Digging!

Spencer Opal Mine
(208) 374-5476

Hotels/Motels
Comfort Inn   Amenities: G,H,R   Cost: *
SR 33
Rexburg, ID 83440
(208) 221-2222

Howard Johnson Hotel   Amenities: H,R,S,NS   Cost: *
1399 Bench Road
Pocatello, ID 83201
(208) 237-1400

NORTHWEST

Legacy Training Camp

There is an unusual concept here; if you can train a chicken, you can train a dog. So they give you this chicken and after several daily sessions, you show your bird off at a competition. Freestyle training and tricks are taught . The campers train their chickens with cracked corn combined with a clicker to remind them of the treat they're given. You remember Pavlov's chicken? Well these babies are amazing! Agility competitions, chickens that give interviews, count to three, dance on command, etc.

This ends up being a great way to teach operant conditioning (reward conditioning) to people that otherwise might use cruel collars, yelling, or yanking on the leash to train their dog. Chickens have no collars, leashes, and yelling doesn't work. (Wonder if this would work with wayward parents who need skills to raise their children...hmmmm?)

Lots of exciting speakers, lectures, dog interaction, and fun await everyone who comes. You don't need to have a dog, but if you bring him there is plenty of fun stuff for the two of you to do. Based in Idaho, the camp is like Paris, a moveable feast. It can be found in any of the 50 states, but only meets once a year. The next one is in Hawaii, but you can't bring your dog for the same reason that I don't list Hawaii in this guide; QUARANTINE! Wait for the next stateside venture, I think Ohio is up next.

Canine Behavior and Training Camp
Moscow, Idaho

Web site: http://www.maui.net/troydog/index.html

Legacy
Terry Ryan
NW 2025 Friel St.
Pullman, WA 99163
(509) 332-2831

Montana

Sights/Towns To See

Glacier National Park
Lake McDonald was the site of one of the "Beethoven" (the dog) movies. Water Sports, hiking, birding and all kinds of outdoor activities are accessible to you and your pet. There are restrictions, so check the area you intend to visit. A park almost unparalled in beauty, it will provide wonderful restful scenery for your vacation.

Glacier National Park
(602) 207-6000
Montana Travel Association
(800) 847-4868

Hotels/Motels
Quality Inn   Amenities: R   Cost: **
920 Spokane Ave.
Whitefish, MT 59937
(406) 862-7600

East Glacier Motel   Amenities: N/A   Cost: *
P.O. Box 93
East Glacier Park, MT 59434
(406) 226-5593

Festivals/Happenings

Buzzard Day
Glendive
A celebration of the return of the "Buzzards" (Turkey Vultures) to Makoshika State Park every spring. Buzzards, for those of you who just said "Oh, gross!", are very important to different ecosystems as the clean-up crew. They don't kill and eat live creatures; they dispose of already dead ones. This removes a large amount of detritus from the land and is a good natural recycling program. Besides, as the top of the

(non-polluting) members of the food chain, they can alert us to dangers from heavy use of agricultural chemicals because they absorb so much. There are 10K, 5K, and 1 mile runs as well as birding, nature walks, hiking, and good food. Leashed pets are welcome.

Theatre in the Park
Glendive
A good 45-minute concert by the community concert choir starts off this evening. Then a 3-piece chicken dinner is served. After this comes the performance of the troupe's choice of melodrama for the evening. All the players are local. Fido can enjoy the whole thing.

Makoshika State Park
1301 Snyder Ave.
Glendive, MT 59330
(406) 365-6256

Hotels/Motels
Jordan Inn   Amenities: R,S,NS   Cost: **
223 N. Merrill
Box 741
Glendive, MT 59330
(406) 365-5655
(800) 824-5067

Kings Inn   Amenities: R,S,NS   Cost: *
1903 N. Merrill
Box 296
Glendive, MT 59330
(406) 365-5636

Mission Mountain Testicle Festival
Charlo
Yup, you heard right! You call 'em "mountain oysters", we call 'em "testicles". It's a festival that has no peer in this guide. The ranchers do the castration in the spring and save these babies for the right event. A big testicle fry; I'll bet you can't eat just one! The dog is invited. I wonder what he'd say if he could talk?

(I had intended to say that if you're bored of the Freeman ranch tour and Ted's Unacastle, there are lots of other things to do in Montana, but I decided not to.)

Hotels/Motels
Allentown Motel & Restaurant   Amenities: R   Cost: *
41000 US 93
Charlo, MT 59824
(406) 644-2588

Sunset Motel   Amenities: NS   Cost: *
32670 US 93
St. Ignatius, MT 59865
(406) 745-3900

Oregon

Sights/Towns To See

Portland
Home to the Tom McCall Waterfront Park where all kinds of pet-friendly festivals take place every month of the year, Portland is a lovely and civilized city. See Mills End Park, the smallest city park in the world (2 feet across!) and Forest Park, the largest city park in America (4000+ acres!). Dogs and cats welcome.

Portland Visitors Association
(503) 275-9750

Hotels/Motels
Comfort Inn   Amenities: G,R,S,T   Cost**
431 N.E. Multnomah
Portland, OR 97232
(503) 233-7933

Howard Johnson Hotel   Amenities: A,R,S,NS   Cost**
7101 N.E. 82nd Avenue
Portland, OR 97220
(503) 255-6722

Mt. Hood National Forest
Drive the state highway loop around Mt. Hood, through the Columbia Gorge, and along the Clackamas River for some relaxing scenic moments. Hike the 1,100 miles of trails, all of which are pet-friendly and include Salmon River, Mirror Lake, and Eagle Creek Trails. There are even "Snow Play" areas in the winter! Go back to childhood and play in the snow! Or ski downhill or cross-country at one of the several ski areas on Mt. Hood terrain.

Mt. Hood National Forest
Gresham, OR
(503) 666-0700

John Day Fossil Beds National Monument
Kimberly Area
Amazing plant and animal fossils found in this area are set out for your perusal. This is not a place where you can harvest your own fossils but the hiking is great. Take only pictures, leave only footprints. It gets hot so make sure your cat, dog, or whatever (they're pretty flexible here) has plenty of water.

John Day Fossil Beds National Monument
HCR 82/ Box 126
Kimberly, OR 97848
(541) 987-2333

House of Mystery Vortex
Gold Hill
The phenomenon that gave the house its name circles the house with a 180 ft diameter force field that is half above and half below ground. The house itself is unusually crooked, and as you head toward the center of the Vortex or toward magnetic North, you visibly lose height. The dog appears shorter too! There is nowhere in the circle that you can stand naturally erect! Cool!

House of Mystery Vortex
4303 Sardine Creek Rd.
Gold Hill, OR 97525
(541) 855-1543

Hillcrest Vineyard
Roseburg
The varietal winery to visit in Oregon, they answered my "Are pets allowed at the winery?" with, "Of course, we love dogs!" A nice, friendly place with a vineyard to roam, party facilities, volleyball court, and picnic tables for your enjoyment.

Hillcrest Vineyard
Roseburg, OR
(541) 673-3709

NORTHWEST

Girardet Wine Cellars
While you're in Roseburg, you can find Girardet Wine Cellars, who sponsor an **Anniversary Fest** in June and a **Barrel Tour Fest** in March. Pets are allowed on the premises to picnic and relax with you. This winery offers beers as well.

Girardet Wine Cellars
895 Reston Rd.
Roseburg, OR 97470
(541) 679-7252

Henry Winery
Umpqua
"Henry Goes Wines" is the name of the great late summer/early fall festival at this pet-friendly vineyard. Free barrel samples, free glass and wine with admission, barbeque, and special discounts make this festival worth attending. Pets might be allowed in the tasting room or touring with you if they are well behaved, and are definitely allowed in the back area outside (which is covered). Rover will have a good time, but remember he is always a non-drinker of alcoholic beverages!

Henry Winery
687 Hubbard Creek Rd.
Umpqua, OR 97486
(541) 459-5120

Gold Beach
Located at the mouth of the Rogue River on the ocean, Gold Beach is ideal for walking with the pooch. Hike the Schrader Forest nearby. There are Rogue River boating, white-water rafting and canoeing tours, but none of them allow dogs. Dog Gone newsletter (see "Publications") has mentioned that Mail-Boat Hydro-Jets and Jerry's Hydro-Jets allow pets, but they must be in the small kennels on board.

Gold Beach Chamber of Commerce
(800) 525-2334

Coos Bay/Charleston Area
Did you see "Twister" or "The Wizard of Oz"? If the prospect of following developing storms excites you as much as it does me, you'll love this area by the ocean! You can follow storms without even moving! In the State Parks there are storm-watching pavilions for your safe perusal of nature's wrath. Whale-watching, and exploring the rocks and beach for creatures can also provide great pleasure.

Bay Area Chamber of Commerce
(800) 824-8486

Festivals/Happenings

The Rose Festival
Portland
Tom McCall Waterfront Park is the site for a lot of exciting festivals including the Rose Festival. There are rides, food concessions and a series of parades of the different rose categories; The Starlight, Junior, and Grand Floral parades. Rides and activities are available as well.

The Annual Waterfront Blues Festival
Portland
Pets are allowed as local and imported musicians strut their stuff by the water. There is just about any type of blues that you can think of at this concert. Again activities, food concessions abound.

Portland Visitors Association
(503) 275-9750

Southern Oregon Kite Festival
Brookings
A two day event with lots of exciting and colorful entries to watch with Fido, or participate in. Make your own, rent or buy a kite for the festival.

Brookings Harbor Chamber of Commerce
(800) 535-9469

Hotels/Motels

Hojo Inn   Amenities: A,H,NS   Cost: *
525 So. Riverside
Medford, OR 97501
(541) 772-6133

Howard Johnson Lodge   Amenities: A,H,R,NS   Cost: *
978 NE Stephen
Roseburg, OR 97470
(541) 673-5082

Friendship Inn   Amenities: G,H,R   Cost: *
390 Broadway
Winchester Bay, OR
(541) 271-4871

Camping Information Center
(503) 731-3411
(800) 452-5687

Oregon State Parks
(503) 378-6305

Dog Friendly State Parks
Sunset Bay State Park /Charleston
Cape Arago State Park /Charleston
Boardman State Park /Brookings
Lone Ranch State Park /Brookings
Dunes National Recreation Area/North Bend
Schrader Forest/Gold Beach
Loeb State Park/Brookings
Harris Beach State Park/Brookings
Whaleshead State Park/Brookings
Azalea Park/Brookings

Dog Friendly Beaches
Oregon State Parks Beaches (All)

Washington

Sights/Towns To See

Seattle

The Seattle area offers some of the best hiking, mountaineering, and water sports of anywhere in the country. Take your pooch on the ferry to the art colony on beautiful Bainbridge Island. A 30-minute trip that gives you incredible views of volcanic, snow-covered Mt. Rainier, you'll also see the Space needle from the ship. After returning from your boating, visit Pike Place Market and shop in clever kiosks for anything and everything. Think about Frazier and Eddie as you stroll around looking for Cafe Nervosa. Write me if you actually find it. I'll send for help. Great little cafes, restaurants, and take-out places can be found here too.

Hotels/Motels

Bainbridge Inn
9200 Hemlock Ave. NE
Bainbridge, WA 98110
(206) 842-7564
Amenities: H   Cost: N/A

Monarch Manor
7656 Yeomalt Pt. Dr. NE
Bainbridge Island, WA 98110
(206) 780-0112
Amenities: SA   Cost:***

The Warwick Hotel
401 Lenora St.
Seattle, WA 98121
(206) 443-4300
Amenities: R,S,H   Cost:***

Spokane

The Arbor Crest Wine Cellars is a breathtaking stop in Spokane even if you're not into wine. But it's a delight if you are. There are regular tastings daily at this historic Riblet Mansion which has a spectacular cliff house tasting room and ample manicured grounds for you to roam.

They also have 2 dogs themselves and respectfully ask that your pet be under control or leashed. You may enjoy a picnic lunch with your wine on the grounds. Play checkers on the giant checker board in the back lawn. The pieces are big enough to require two hands to lift!

Hotels/Motels
Spokane Bed & Breakfast   Amenities: S,R   Cost**
Reservation Service
E. 627 25th Ave.
Spokane, WA 99203
(509) 624-3776

Apple Tree Inn Motel   Amenities: H,S,R,NS   Cost**
N. 9508 Division
Spokane, WA 99203
(800) 323-5796

Cavanaugh's River Inn   Amenities: H,S,R,NS   Cost**
700 N. Division
Spokane, WA 99202
(800) THE-INNS

Granger/ Yakima Valley
If you are an oenophile and want to see the entire state of Washington's wineries, start at the Hyatt Vineyards in the Yakima valley. They have a spectacular view of Mt. Rainier and Mt. Adams, A large windmill, 80 acres of grapes, and a very special black muscat (if you're into "muscat love"). Lots of folks have their weddings here and they are happy for you to bring your pet and picnic and taste on the grounds.

Hotels/Motels
Llama Ranch B&B   Amenities: R   Cost:**
1980 Highway 141
White Salmon, WA 98672

Bali Hai Motel   Amenities: R,S,NS   Cost:**
710 N. 1st St.
Yakima, WA 98901
(509) 452-7178

Colonial Motor Inn   Amenities: R,S,NS   Cost:**
1405 N. 1st St.
Yakima, WA 98901
(509) 453-8981

Dog Friendly Beaches
Long Beach/Long Beach
Ocean Shores/Mid-coast
Westport Beaches/Mid-coast
Grayland Beaches/Mid-coast
Rialto Beach/Olympic Nat'l. Park
Hole-in-the-Wall/Olympic Nat'l Park
All Washington State Park Beaches

Wyoming

Sights/Towns To See

Yellowstone National Park
Not the "Jellystone" Park of Yogi Bear; it is rare to see black bear here today (they're being "managed"), but you can still see elk, bison and other wild creatures in this vast and beautiful wilderness where your pet is welcomed if on a leash.   Beautiful waterfalls, geysers, and unparalled natural beauty await the traveler.

Yellowstone National Park
P.O. Box 168
Yellowstone, WY 82190
(307) 344-7381

Hotels/Motels
Coachman Inn   Amenities: S   Cost*
112 Hwy 20
S. Yellowstone, WY
(307) 864-3141

Lander (in the South Pass area)
A lifelong Wyoming resident told me that if she'd had her druthers, she'd take the Oregon Trail outside of Lander and look for the several ghost towns that are largely unexplored around that area. Sounds like great fun! There's also an old gold mine awaiting the travelers' careful exploration.

Lander Chamber of Commerce
160 N. 1st St.
Lander, WY 82520
(307) 332-3892

Hotels/Motels
MacKenzie Highland Ranch   Amenities: R   Cost: N/A
3945 Highway 26
Dubois, WY 82513
(307)-455-3415
Pets in cabins only

Fossil Butte/ Kemmerer
Fossil Butte is considered a National Forest, with all the trappings of flora and fauna that one would expect to find in this part of Wyoming. Pets on leash are welcome in this 8000+ acre park. The Kemmerer area is of great interest to those with an archeological bent because there are sponsored digs of areas with known fossils. Take care not to remove any fossils (or anything else for that matter) from Fossil Butte proper, though. Although it is in Kemmerer, it is still a National Park and all matter living or dead belongs to we-the-collective people, not we-the-individual people.

Fossil Butte
Box 592
Kemmerer, WY 83101
(307) 877-4455

Kemmerer Chamber of Commerce
800 Pine
Kemmerer, WY 83101
(307) 877-9761

Hotels/Motels
Fossil Butte Motel   Amenities: N/A   Cost*
1424 Central Ave.
Kemmerer, WY 83101
(307) 877-3996

Lake Viva Naughton Marina Motel   Amenities: R Cost*
Hwy 233
Kemmerer, WY 83101
(307) 877-9669

NORTHWEST

Great Drives in Wyoming

Bighorn National Forest
Get in the car and go from Sheridan to Tongue River over the Bighorn mountains. Drop into Shell Canyon and see the rapid falls shoot down into the basin. Breathtaking.

Highway 130
The scenic Highway 130 passes through Centennial and the wildflowers on either side of the road are spectacular.

Main Road/Thermopolis
Take the main road from Thermopolis to Shoshoni, the scenery is Wyoming-lovely. Thermopolis is home to (all you etymologists already guessed) the famous hot springs and the Hot Springs County Fair (August). Take a dip-could change your outlook!

Hotels/Motels

Cactus Inn Motel 605 S. 6th Thermopolis, WY (307) 864-3155	Amenities: N/A	Cost*
Coachman Inn 112 Hwy 20 S. Yellowstone, WY (307) 864-3141	Amenities: N/A	Cost*
Foothills Ranch B&B 521 Pass Creek Rd. Parkman, WY 82838 (307) 655-9362	Amenities: N/A	Cost**

CANADA

Sights/Towns To See

Vancouver/Victoria, British Columbia
Dog friendly beaches stretch for miles along the Pacific coast and it's an easy hop from Seattle on a pet-friendly ferry. Acres and acres of woodlands are yours to explore. Visit the Stanley Park seawall to see lots of dog owners and their charges. The shopping is fun here too!

Regal Empress Hotel   Amenities:R   Cost:****
721 Government St.
Victoria, BC V8W 1WS
(800) 828-7447

Westin Bayshore   Amenities:R   Cost:****
1601 W. Georgia St.
Vancouver, BC V6G 2V4
(604) 682-3377

The Four Seasons   Amenities:R   Cost:****
Vancouver, BC V6G 2V4
(602) 689-9333

Hotel Douglas   Amenities:R   Cost:****
Victoria, BC V8W 1WS
(602) 383-4157

Jandana Ranch   Amenities: R   Cost: ***
Pinantan Lake, BC VOE 3EO
(604) 573-5800
3 Pets per cabin (inside)

Hitch & Rail   Amenities: R   Cost: **
P.O. Box 115
Heffley Creek, BC VOE 1ZO
(604) 578-7112 (Pets allowed in cabins)

Festivals/Happenings

Agility and Flyball Tournament
Edmonton, Alberta
If Flyball is your game, or you just want to teach the pooch a new trick, head for the **Agility and Flyball Tournament** in Edmonton in August. (See "Pets On The Net" in the back for two Flyball web sites). If not, just go and watch the fur fly...

Hotels/Motels
Howard Johnson Plaza   Amenities:R,S   Cost:***
10010 104th St.
Edmonton, AB T5J OZ1

Great Manitoba Dog Party
Winnipeg, Manitoba
The **"Great Manitoba Dog Party"** takes place just north of Winnipeg. Almost 16,000 people and 1,000 dogs gather each year for a series of events, dog product displays, look-alike contests and much more. Almost all Ontario and Manitoba National Parks accept dogs and lots of businesses cater to them.

Tulip Festival
Ottawa, Ontario
Don't miss the **Tulip Festival** in May (pet-friendly, of course). A gathering together of all those who appreciate the finest examples of this, our waxiest flower. They're stunningly beautiful because they're so waxy. I hope you've seen the "I Love Lucy" episode where she tries to win the tulip competition with fake, wax tulips. A priceless television moment.

Hotels/Motels
Ramada Hotel & Suites   Amenities: H,R,NS   Cost: **
111 Cooper St.
Ottawa, ON K2P 2E3
(613) 238-1331

PET-FRIENDLY RESOURCE GUIDE

This list of resources has been assembled for any additional needs that pet owners might have which have not been addressed in the body of the text. These include the following:

Pet Travel Publications
Pet Products
Pet-Related Services and Clubs
Pets On The Net

This information is followed by a section of special offers provided by pet-friendly establishments across the country.

Pet Publications

Take Your Pet Along ($14.95 + $3.00 S&H)
This publication covers the entire U.S. and Canada and includes advice, travel tips, amenities, hotels, motels, and some B&B's. It is currently the most economical guide on the market.
(See order form in the back)
MCE
P.O. Box 84
Chester, NJ 07930
(908) 879-7564

The Dogs' Guide To New York City ($14.95 + S&H)
This wonderful guide lists dog friendly department stores such as F.A.O. Schwarz, Bloomingdales, etc. There are several dog friendly restaurants listed as well. Dog clothiers, bookstores and hotels are listed.
Jack's City Dog Publcations
Richmond Press
(800) 560-1560

DogGone Newsletter ($24.00 for 6 Issues- 1 year)
A bimonthly publication with ideas, recipes, interesting outings and advice about all aspects of pet travel, DogGone is worth looking into.
DogGone
P.O. Box 651155
Vero Beach, FL 32965

On The Road Again With MAN'S BEST FRIEND ($14.95 for each section (e.g. New England)
A very entertaining guide, it describes in great detail all of the amenities of each featured hotel or inn. Worth getting for specific details about places to stay with your pet.
Dawbert Press
P.O. Box 2758
Duxbury, MA 02331
(800) 93-DAWBERT

Vacationing With Your Pet : Eileen's Directory of Pet Friendly Lodging ($19.95)
Many hotels, motels, and B&B's are found in this guide. Eileen also has valuable phone numbers, pet safety tips, and discussions of non-travel subjects. A valuable resource. She's also got "Doin' California With Your Pooch", a great hiking guide.

Pet-Friendly Publications
P.O. Box 8459
Scottsdale, AZ 85252
(800) 496-2665

Pets-R-Permitted: Hotel, Motel, Kennel & Petsitter ($12.95)
This guide has campgrounds as well as hotels and motels. Also listed are pet resorts, a unique inclusion in these guidebooks, as well as a helpful zipcode guide to accomodations near the town in which you wish to stay.

Purchase Registration
P.O. Box 11374
Torrance, CA 90510
(310) 374-6246

Take Your Pet USA ($11.95)
In its sixth printing, this guide lists hotels, motels, and special amenities for pets like exercise areas. It is a pocket guide with some coupons for travel.

Artco
12 Channel St.
Boston, MA 02210
(800) 255-8038

California Dog Lovers' Companion
This helpful guide to hotels and motels in California lists two dozen hotels in the San Diego area alone. This book includes many unexpected places to stay. The manager of the San Diego Princess, for example, has a very common sense attitude about pets and allows them in his wonderful resort. Worth getting.

(213) 730-5323

Pet Products

Protect-A-Pet Seat Belt
June Enterprises
P.O. Box 180
1658 Matterson Rd.
Errington, B.C. Canada V0R 1V0
(604) 248-7345 ($28-38)

CycleTote (To carry doggie behind on bike trips)
CycleTote Corp.
517 N. Link Ln.
Ft. Collins, CO 80524
(800) 747-2407
(303) 482-2401

Sherpa Pet Bags
Foster & Smith
(800) 826-7200

Le Pet Bag
Foster & Smith
(800) 826-7200

Pet-Pak First Aid Kit
Aftercare, Inc.
P.O. Box 982
Edison, NJ 08818
(908) 906-9200

Pet Shade (available in "Mutt Hut" amd "Sun Snoozer" models)
Gale Group
Apopka, FL
(800) 325-8790

Cool Paws (booties to protect pets' paws from hot surfaces)
(800) 650-PAWS or (602) 968-4491

Pet-Related Services and Clubs

Pet Travel Consultant
Katrina Weiner
(916) 536-9859
(800) 205-0406
Trip packages are $25/city or $75/trip.
Includes maps and hotels.

Pet Care Savings Club
4501 Forbes Blvd.
Lanham, MD 20706
(800) 388-6978
(800) 388-7387
For $49.95 a year you receive 50% off all your pet-friendly hotels.
You also get a hotel directory, a 24-hour hotline for pet health and
behavior, "ANIMALOCATOR" tags for your furry friend, and benefits
which could save you up to $350 a year (in pet care products, car
rentals, etc.) And you can cancel anytime.

Hugs & Kisses Newsletter
A quarterly newsletter with a wealth of excellent information on
training, feeding and caring for your pets by the world-renowned
expert, Warren Eckstein. Nobody knows your pet better. A big plus is
that this helps support the Hugs & Kisses Fund, a non-profit
organization dedicated to Warren's loving wife who devoted her life to
preventing animal suffering. This fund helps out all of the small, hard-
working organizations that have limited resources and do much good
work. Only $24.95/year. Write or call today.

Hugs & Kisses Newsletter
2633 Lincoln Blvd. Suite 230
Santa Monica, CA 90405
(800) 430-4847

Dog Square Dancing
Promenade Pups (Dallas County)
Woofing Hoofers (Simsbury, CT)
Create a club in your town!

Country Dance & Song Society (Music)
(413) 584-9913
United Square Dancers of America (Steps)
(205) 881-6044

Dog Lover's Dating Service
(For *you,* not your dog)
Dog Lover's Junction
P.O. Box 56
Highland, MD 20777-0056

American Kennel Club
5580 Centerview Dr.
Raleigh, NC 27690-0643
Information   (919) 233-9767
Administration (212) 696-8200

Pet Sitters
Pet Sitters International
(800) 268-SITS

National Association of Professional Pet Sitters
(800) 296-7387

Kritter Sitters
Mar Vista, CA
(310) 398-8148

B&B for DOG
Denver, CO
(303) 745-8538

The Dog House
Doggie Day Care
Los Angeles, CA
(213) 549-WOOF

Pets on the Net

Travel Info / Take Your Pet Along
http://www.world2u.com/pettravel

The Pet Channel
http://www.thepetchannel.com

Save-A-Pet On-Line
http://www.pasture.ecn.purdue.edu/~laird/Dogs/Rescue/
http://www.tezcat.com

Starting a Purebred Rescue
http://www.cyberpet.com/cyberdog/rescue/reschow.html

Canine FAQ's
http://www.zmall.com/pet_talk/dog-faqs/homepage.html

The Canine Web
http://www.snapple.cs.washington.edu/canine/canine.html

Medical Info
http://www.zoo.vet.cornell.edu/~dlm7/canine.html

Dog Owner's Guide
http://www.canismajor.com/dog/guide.html

Pet Loss & Grieving Resources
http://www.cowpoke.com/~twscan/Pet.html

Fleas and Ticks
http://www.zmall.com/pet_talk/petfaqs/fleas-ticks.html

Cat Fanciers' Association
http://www.cfainc.org

Feline Information Page
http://www.best.com/~sirlou/cat.shtml

Interpet
http://vanbc.wimsey.com/~dmtaylor/interpet/ip_pages.html

Pet Station
http://www.petstation.com

Internet Cat Club
http://www.taylsntufts.com/~icc

International Cat Association
http://www.tica.org

Cat Fanciers Mailing List
http://www.fanciers.com

Dr. Jim's Virtual Cat Clinic
http://www.rampages.onramp.net:80/~drjim

A Tale of Two Kitties
http://www.twokitties.com

The IAMS Company
http://www.iamsco.com

Acme Pet
http://www.acmepet.com

Dog Food Recipe Homepage
http://www.iinet.net.au/~daoimage/dog.html

Dog Breeder's Network
http://www.breeders.com

People For The Ethical Treatment of Animals
http://envirolink.org/arrs/peta

Grooming Homepage
http://webz.com/madson/

Flyball Homepage
http://www.cs.umn.edu/~ianhogg/flyball/flyball.html

Flyball Homepage
http://dspace.dial.pipex.com/town/square/tac61/flyball.htm

The International Superdogs show schedule
http://www.geocities.com/hollywood/3155/

Flying Disc Homepage
http://www.vais.net/~krobair/discdog.html

The AKC National Breed Clubs
http://www.akc.org/akc/bredclub.htm

The NETVET
http://netvet.wustl.edu/dogs.htm

Figure/Picture Legend

TURTLE BEACH RESORT
9049 Midnight Pass Road • Tel (941) 349-4554
Fax (941) 918-0203

"The romantic hidden jewel of Siesta Key," a charming waterfront Inn. Tropical and peaceful bayfront cottages/villas, each with private spa, patio and distinctive decor: "Victorian", "Key West", etc. All the comforts of home in fully equipped studios & 2 Br cottages. Spectacular bay views, inground pool, lush landscaping, gazebo, secluded sunsets on Turtle Beach. Gourmet waterfront dining next door. Paddleboats, fishing, watersports, bicycles. **PETS Welcome**

Cypress Inn
Carmel-By-The-Sea, California

CYPRESS INN

Lincoln & 7th Sts.
P. O. Box Y
Carmel, CA 93921

408/624-3871
800/443-7443

Fax: 408/624-8216

Doris Day welcomes you and your pet(s) to visit this historic property located within steps of all the shops, restaurants & galleries of Carmel-by-the-Sea!

WE LOVE YOUR PETS, TOO!

RHODE ISLAND'S PREMIERE HOTEL
FEATURING:
INDOOR POOL & HEALTH CENTER
WALKING PATH
COMPLIMENTARY AIRPORT SHUTTLE
FULL SERVICE RESTAURANT
LOUNGE
EXTRA LARGE ROOMS
BEAUTIFULLY MANICURED GROUNDS

EXIT 12A OFF INTERSTATE 95
801 GREENWICH AVENUE
WARWICK, RI 02886
401-732-6000
OR 800-HOLIDAY

Visit the Wonderful New Jersey Shore!
Stay with the Best!
The New England Motel!!

Newly Renovated Resort Motel
Also a house that sleeps 18!
Discounts to area businesses
Casino bus at door
Weight room nearby
Laundry facilities
Barbeque at poolside
Clean, comfortable atmosphere

Call

(609) 522-7250
(800) 9UT-MAID
In Winter, (609) 428-9662

Discount Special
5% off a 2 night stay (or more)
when you mention this ad.

1667 1756

Great Places to Stay

BEST 17TH-CENTURY GETAWAY

Much of THE STEPHEN DANIELS HOUSE dates from 1667, and the furnishings include some very early antiques. Kay Gill has owned the house since 1962, taking in guests long before B&Bs were a concept in Salem. Several of the five guest rooms have working hearths, and those in the common room and original kitchen are huge. Guests can relax in the kitchen, the parlor, and dining room or in the pleasant garden with flowering shrubbery and wisteria. Children are welcome and so (surprisingly) are pets.

The Stephen Daniels House
One Daniels Street
Salem, Massachusetts 01970

THE HILLTOP INN
Route 117, Sugar Hill, NH 03585
800-770-5695 / 603-823-5695
Fax 603-823-5518
Email mike.hern@hilltopinn.com

1895 Victorian nestled in the peaceful village of Sugar Hill in the heart of the White Mountains. A romantic escape offering large breakfasts, comfortable guest rooms, suites and a cottage all filled with antiques, handmade quilts and immaculate private baths. Relax on our porches or by a crackling fire. Stroll down quiet country roads with spectacular mountain views. We are 10 minutes from Franconia Notch. **Pets very welcomed.** AAA ◆◆◆ MC, VISA, DISCOVER
The Hilltop Inn has been featured in *Yankee, Outside, Country Victorian, Boston Globe* and numerous travel guides.

CENTENNIAL·INN
FARMINGTON
All-Suite Conference Facility

The home away from home
for you & your pet!

$94*

Spacious **One Bedroom Suite** featuring fully-equipped kitchens and living room with cable tv/vcr;

Complimentary deluxe **continental breakfast** served da featuring fresh baked bagels, french toast, hot & cold cereals, mini-pastries, coffee, tea, decaff & juices;

12 wooded acres for you & your pet to explore.

*Rates are per night and based on availability. Rates do not include 12% CT State Occupancy Tax.

For Reservations...contact the Sales Department **1-800-852-2052**

5 Spring Lane, Farmington, CT 06032
860/677-4647 • Resv. 800/852-2052 • Fax 860/676-0685
Professionally Managed by **Konover** *Hotel Corporation.*

Woodbury
Motel & Apts.

407 Surf Ave.
N. Wildwood, NJ 08260
1½ Blocks To Beach

The Woodbury is your place.
Your pet is our *Very Special Guest*.
10% off any stay at the Woodbury
if you mention that you read this special book.

Reservations
Office
(609) 522-7315

NJ Pets

Show this ad and receive
1 free pig ear or 2" fur mouse cat toy!
Limit one per ad.
Good one time only.

The ISAAC RANDALL HOUSE

Comfortable, antique-furnished rooms, all with private bath and telephone, each with its own decor. Some rooms have working fireplaces; others offer cable TV-VCRs. In summer, every sleeping room is air conditioned for your comfort. FAX service is also available, and for the pleasure of our smaller guests, there's a great playground on our six wooded acres with spring-fed pond. We're within easy walking distance of downtown Freeport.

Enjoy a hearty breakfast and lively conversation in our charming, beam-ceilinged country kitchen, before starting the day. In the evening, relax in our common area where complimentary snacks are available. Books and parlor games are provided for your enjoyment, as are cable TV and VCR.

Mention this ad for $10 off on off-peak season.
Special Packages available for multiple stays.
Honeymoon, Off-season, etc.
Triple A three diamond rated.

Freeport, ME - (207) 865-9295

HOWL-O-WEEN HIKE

Sunday, October 27, 1996
12 noon to 4 pm
Rain or Shine
North Branch Park
Milltown Road
Bridgewater, NJ

For more
information
call
201-514-
5888

Two-Mile
Noncompetitve Walk,
Canine Contest and
Activities,
Entertainment, Food,
Prizes

Walk your dog to benefit St. Hubert's Giralda
Animal Welfare and Education Center and its
important programs for animals and people.

Clip here

$1 OFF REGISTRATION FEE

*Redeem this coupon for one dollar off the Howl-o-ween Hike
registration fee.*

Valid through October 27, 1996

WHEN WAS THE LAST TIME
YOU AND YOUR DOG SAVED A LIFE?

:°: DOGS WALK
AGAINST CANCER

WHAT? A non-competitive dog walk-athon to raise money for the fight against human & animal cancers

FOR WHOM? The American Cancer Society with a portion of the net proceeds to be donated to the Animal Medical Center (Donaldson-Atwood Cancer Clinic)

CALL FOR REGISTRATION INFORMATION FOR A TAIL-WAGGING GOOD TIME

THE AMERICAN CANCER SOCIETY • 212/237-3872

Wheeling, West Virginia
Comfort Inn

Escape to the one Wheeling-area hotel that combines the best of both worlds - the serenity of a scenic, hilltop setting with the convenience of easy access to Wheeling's many attractions!

I-70, Exit 11
Wheeling, WV 26003
304-547-1380

Comfort Inn

Pets stay free if you mention this ad!

Bob Bates Illustrator

14023 SUNSET DR.,
WHITTIER, CALIF. 90602

PHONE (310) 693-8101
FAX (310) 693-0460

Give The Gift Of Fun: A Year Of DogGone!

[ ] Hey, I want my friends the discover fun places to go and do cool stuff with their dog! Enter a gift subscription for 1 year (6 issues of **DogGone**™) for just $24.00. (For gifts to Florida residents, add $1.44 state sales tax.)

Name _____

Address_____

City _____ State _____ Zip _____

Dog's Name(s)_____

Breed(s) _____

[ ] Gift Subscription from_____

Mail this coupon with check or M.O. payable to DogGone to: **DogGone**, P.O. Box 651155, Vero Beach, FL 32965-1155.

Personalized Travel Information

AN EXCLUSIVE SERVICE FOR DOGGONE SUBSCRIBERS

Name _____

Address_____

City _____ State _____ Zip _____

Telephone (_____) _____

I'd like information on _____ (city or state).

Additional city(ies) or state(s) _____

_____ (Enclose $10.00 each)

Accommodations Preference:

[ ] Bed & Breakfast/Inn   [ ] Farm/Ranch   [ ] Resort

[ ] Campground/RV Park   [ ] Hotel/Motel   [ ] All

Month/Date of Planned Trip_____

Mail coupon to P.O. Box 651155, Vero Beach, FL 32965-1155.
PHOTOCOPIES NOT ACCEPTED. ORIGINAL COUPON MUST BE MAILED.

MCE Press
P.O. Box 84 Chester, NJ 07930
Phone (908) 879-7564 (800) 932-3017
Email DocMacLean @ aol.com

The Books We Offer:

Nobody's Best Friend by Lorraine Houston
Twelve touching stories of shelter dogs who Lorraine Houston, a world-class dog motivator, has worked with in her lifetime of fostering and caring for dogs. It also includes an Appendix with terrific training techniques (some never seen before!) and practical sections like Adopting A Shelter Dog, The Lure Method, The Language Barrier, Entertainment, The Kong Trick, Preventing Unwanted Behaviour, and Housetraining.
(140pp) Retail Price $12.95 Spiral Trade Paperback (1999) ISBN 09648913-60

Take Your Pet Along-1001 Places To Stay by Heather MacLean Walters
A comprehensive reference to all the pet-friendly hotels, motels, and B&B's across the US and Canada. Includes are costs, amenities, pet-friendly travel tips, all pet travel publications, money-saving coupons, clubs, services, and GREAT web sites!
(320 pp.) Retail Price $14.95 Trade Paperback (1997) ISBN 09648913-28

Take Your Pet Too! Fun Things To Do! by Heather MacLean Walters
A unique reference guide to annual events and exciting places. The only nationwide pet-friendly vacation planner on the market, it includes concerts, galas, cruises, beaches, restaurants, festivals, fairs, dog camps, wine-tastings, museums, and much more! Discount coupons included.
(312 pp.) Retail Price $16.95 Trade Paperback (1997) ISBN 09648913-1X

Nutritional Warfare by Dr. Heather MacLean Walters
A comprehensive and revealing guide that will amaze you with new, vital information critical to good, healthy livingand making informed choices. LEARN THE TRUTH about Irradiation, Pesticides, What To Eat, Antioxidants, Who You Can Trust, Cancer Prevention, Deciphering Food Labels, Viruses In Our Food, Mad Cow Disease, Industry Secrets and Much, Much More!!!
(460+pp) Retail Price $ 17.95 Spiral Trade Paperback (1999) ISBN 09648913-36

The Great Antioxidant Lie by Dr. Heather MacLean Walters
We know that antioxidants prevent cancer, and yet we keep hearing new studies that say that a certain ANTIOXIDANT CAUSES CANCER? How can that be? The Great Antioxidant Lie has a common sense hypothesis that could save your life and the lives of your family and friends. Read about topics like: Is Your Cereal KILLING You? Why COFFEE may be your best vitamin! Are there antioxidants in CIGARETTES? Take the new anticancer pill (angiostatin) for almost no cost, with no prescription!!!
(185pp) Retail Price $15.95 Spiral Trade Paperback (1999) ISBN 09648913-44

The Philology Of Taste by Professor Harry Randall
Subtitled "The Wayward Language Of Food", this wonderful coffeetable book explores the relationship of words about food and why we use them. It shows us how the words we use to describe our favorite meals reveal our most personal desires. From *scullery* and the story of *stone soup* to the derivation of *al forno* and *frangipani*, the Professor knows all and tells all.
(135pp) Retail Price $24.95 Hardcover / Illus. (1995)

MCE Book Order Form

Name: _____

Address: _____

City/State/Zip: _____

Phone Number _____

Payment: ☐ Check ☐ Money Order ☐ American Express:

Card Number: _____
Expiration Date: _____

Take Your Pet Along-1001 Places To Stay	$14.95
Hotels, motels, and pet-friendly B&Bs 320pp (1997)	
Take Your Pet Too! Fun Things to Do!	$16.95
Vacation planner w/ fairs, festivals, cruises, etc. 312pp (1997)	
Nobody's Best Friend	$12.95
12 touching tales of shelter dogs who were saved 140pp (1999)	
Nutritional Warfare	$17.95
A comprehensive, revealing guide to preventive eating 460+pp (1999)	
The Great Antioxidant Lie	$15.95
The real truth about antioxidants -both bad and good 185pp (1999)	
The Philology Of Taste	$24.95
An amusing look a the wayward language of food 135pp (1995)	

Receive a 10% discount on two or three books
Receive a 20% discount on any four or more
[Call 800-932-3017 for further bulk discounts]

Total Order	$	.
Shipping & Handling		
($3.00 each book-to $9.00 total for any order/any # books)	$	.
Tax (6% if you are a NJ resident)	$	.
TOTAL	$	.